Praise for *Beyond Poverty and Affluence*

"Bob Goudzwaard and Harry de Lange bring to the subject an engaging mix of academic empiricism, perceptive practicality, and moral responsibility. This book is long overdue. . . . I commend it to English readers everywhere."

—MAURICE F. STRONG
Secretary-General of the 1992 Earth Summit
Chairman of Ontario Hydro

"A powerful and empowering book! Assembling in new ways what we already know of increasing environmental degradation, poverty, and unemployment, *Beyond Poverty and Affluence* not only identifies the underlying causes but also empowers us to act on setting things right."

—CALVIN B. DeWITT
University of Wisconsin–Madison
Director, Au Sable Institute

"May this book force all of us to confront *the* problem of our time: that we are doomed if we hold fast to an economic system based on consumption and unrestricted exploitation of the earth's resources. We must listen to the visionary message of Bob Goudzwaard and Harry de Lange, learn to live with less in our personal lives, and curb industrial growth that contributes to impoverishment and environmental degradation. Our survival depends on an economy that reflects the fundamental need for sustainable development."

—CHRISTINE STEWART, M.P.
Secretary of State (Latin America and Africa), Canada

"Bob Goudzwaard and Harry de Lange bring a vision of realistic hope to a troubled, cynical age. They give the lie to the jaded secular belief that economic growth with an accompanying rise in income will one day automatically reach the ends of the earth and the poorest people therein. I recommend their work enthusiastically. It will challenge laypersons and professionals alike."

—WILLIAM F. RYAN, S.J.
former General Secretary of the Canadian
Conference of Catholic Bishops; founding director,
Center of Concern, Washington, D.C.

"The issues are dealt with convincingly and extensively. This book presents enough ideas to convince us of the importance of pursuing a way of life that not only takes into account the significant problems of the day but also contributes to their solution."

—JAN TINBERGEN
Nobel prize–winning economist

Beyond Poverty and Affluence

Toward an Economy of Care
With a Twelve-Step Program
  for Economic Recovery

by BOB GOUDZWAARD *and* HARRY DE LANGE

With a Foreword by Maurice F. Strong
Secretary-General of the 1992 Earth Summit
Chairman of Ontario Hydro

Translated and Edited by Mark R. Vander Vennen

WILLIAM B. EERDMANS PUBLISHING COMPANY
GRAND RAPIDS, MICHIGAN

WCC PUBLICATIONS
GENEVA

Originally published as *Genoeg van te Veel, Genoeg van te Weinig: Wissels omzetten in de economie*
© 1986 Ten Have, Baarn, the Netherlands
Third edition 1991

English translation © 1995 Wm. B. Eerdmans Publishing Co.
255 Jefferson Ave. S.E., Grand Rapids, Michigan 49503

Published jointly 1995 by Wm. B. Eerdmans and
WCC Publications
World Council of Churches
150 route de Ferney, 1211 Geneva 2, Switzerland

Printed in the United States of America

00 99 98 97 96 95   7 6 5 4 3 2 1

Library of Congress Cataloging-in-Publication Data

Goudzwaard, B.
    [Genoeg van de veel, genoeg van de weinig. English]
    Beyond poverty and affluence: toward an economy of care, with a
twelve-step program for economic recovery / by Bob Goudzwaard and
Harry de Lange; with a foreword by Maurice F. Strong; translated and
edited by Mark Vander Vennen.
        p.   cm.
    Includes bibliographical references.
    ISBN 0-8028-0827-1
    1. Economic policy. 2. Economic development.   I. Lange, H. M. de.
II. Vennen, Mark vander.   III. Title.
HD87.G6813   1994
338.9 — dc20   94-23346
                                                              CIP

WCC Publications ISBN 2-8254-1138-8

Contents

Foreword

The Earth Summit has concentrated the mind wonderfully on these issues.

World Link, magazine of the World Economic Forum

This borrowing from Dr. Samuel Johnson was especially appropriate in describing the United Nations Conference on Environment and Development at Rio de Janeiro in June 1992. It concentrated not only the mind but also the hearts of humankind. It riveted the world's attention on the fragility of Earth's environment and the finiteness of its resources. It illuminated, as never before, in the presence of the largest host of world political leaders ever gathered in one place, the indisputable fact that the global community is on a pathway to destruction.

The full quotation from Dr. Johnson is this: "When a man knows he is to be hanged in a fortnight, it concentrates his mind wonderfully." And though the Earth Summit was not convened under quite such exigent circumstances, it was nevertheless steeped in a sense of urgency and ultimatum. There was a pervasive conviction that if agreement was not achieved, at least in principle, to set in Rio a new, more sustainable, more secure, and more humane course for Planet Earth and its inhabitants, there would be few better chances.

Thus the minds at Rio were concentrated wonderfully — and the critical agreement was reached. It did not go as far as many wanted.

Prime Minister Gro Harlem Brundtland, chair of the United Nations World Commission on Environment and Development, whose prescient report *Our Common Future* was a precursor to the Earth Summit, summed up Rio this way: "Progress in many fields, too little progress in most fields, and no progress at all in some fields." But she added: "I am convinced that we will succeed in standing up to the dangers facing us because there are simply no alternatives."

The Earth Summit was neither a beginning nor an end, and it most assuredly was not a "one-shot" panacea. Certainly the short-term signals of real action are not encouraging. There has been an understandable, albeit regrettable, tendency to lapse back to business as usual, particularly in light of the pressing political and economic concerns that have gripped the world since Rio. It would not be realistic to expect the kind of fundamental changes called for at Rio to emerge quickly or easily.

But there is real basis for hope that the UNCED has laid the foundations for the changes in public attitudes and the political mindset necessary to achieve the transition to sustainable development.

The spirit of Rio burns on undiminished, now more than a year later. Indeed, the Earth Summit has produced a universal dialogue of unheard-of intensity and resolve. The protocols achieved at Rio, along with the Agenda 21 implementation blueprint, are on everyone's agenda, at every level of society and in every corner of the Earth. The issue of sustainable development, which languished as an abstruse and idealistic notion for five years after it was propounded in the Brundtland Report in 1987, now blossomed full-force as an inescapable and crucial imperative.

It is clear that, while governments may be approaching sustainable development with characteristic wariness, ordinary people, in communities and special interest organizations around the world, are not about to let the spirit of Rio die on the vine. They are translating it into a new era of grassroots interest and action that will contribute to the implementation of Agenda 21 and infuse the political process with new energies and fresh resolve.

And that wonderful concentration of minds has, among other things, resulted in a concentration of wonderful minds — as indeed befits a subject of such compelling significance. Among these are Bob Goudzwaard and Harry de Lange, two eminent and probing Dutch economists who bring to the subject an engaging mix of academic empiricism, perceptive practicality, and moral responsibility. My own sense of the human dimension of sustainable development was heightened immeasurably by my fourteen-year association with Dr. de Lange on the Working Committee on Church and Society of the World Council of Churches.

This book, *Beyond Poverty and Affluence: Toward an Economy of Care,* is the long overdue English translation of the authors' work first published in 1986. The third edition was also translated and published in German. Now available in English, it was translated by my esteemed friend Mark Vander Vennen. I commend it to English readers everywhere.

MAURICE F. STRONG

Preface

Beyond Poverty and Affluence: Toward an Economy of Care first surfaced in Dutch in 1986. The impetus for writing the book was our conviction that currently accepted economic practice could not aid in the renewal of society. Events in the intervening years have in no way weakened this conviction. On the contrary, now more than ever, we believe, our society must grapple with several distressing issues: poverty, which is spreading like a cancer in many areas of the world; ominous forms of pollution and environmental degradation; and ongoing losses in both the quantity and quality of work. Together these realities voice an urgent appeal for reflection and for a bold new economic practice.

We offer our deliberations in the hope that our colleagues in economics as well as interested persons and groups in society will respond with constructive criticisms. We also trust that, where necessary, they will improve the proposals for economic recovery outlined in this book. We have drafted these proposals in the hope that a public consensus will emerge in the industrialized nations, a consensus that holds our eyes and ears wide open to the needs of the developing countries, especially to those of the poor living there, and to the interests of future generations.

The twelve-step program for economic recovery proposed in the final chapter demonstrates how alternative reflection about our economy can take on concrete shape. The steps framed there also contain elements of proposals made by other organizations and research bodies. We present them in the hope that the public will exert stronger pressure on our politicians and institutions to begin to implement these and similar proposed steps.

Before we begin, a word is in order about our own personal context. Throughout the book we shall argue that the foundations of our local, national, and international economy require renewal. In this we have been influenced by the exchange of ideas occurring in the area of social ethics in the ecumenical community. Both of us are members of Christian churches in the Netherlands and serve on the Dutch Council of Churches' "Working Group on Church and Society." The ecumenical world, in concert with the efforts of the World Council of Churches, is attempting to link more closely a personal and collective faith commitment with the day-to-day activities of those who profess that faith, not only socially and culturally, but also economically. Those working in the ecumenical context have also subjected their reflections to theoretical scrutiny, recognizing, for example, that the specific concept of "justice" they adopt will have a marked impact on whatever efforts they may make to promote justice in an often unjust world.

After several years of dialogue, we decided in 1986 to publish our reflections and proposals jointly. In 1990 a German translation and edition of the book appeared, an edition that is now used in discussion groups especially in the eastern part of Germany. In 1991 a third, revised and expanded Dutch edition was published. Now, thinking of an English-speaking and more international audience, we have made further revisions.

Finally, we wish to express publicly our heartfelt gratitude to the many friends whose efforts have led to the publication of this English edition. We particularly wish to thank Maurice Strong for his gracious contribution of the Foreword to the book. We also especially wish to thank Gerald Vandezande, who kindly read the English text and offered valuable suggestions, and Mark Vander Vennen, our translator and editor, who deserves an Oscar for his patience and endurance!

BOB GOUDZWAARD
HARRY DE LANGE

CHAPTER 1

Why Economic Renewal?

In this book we shall attempt to demonstrate that our economy has reached the point where it must be fundamentally renewed. We shall argue that our economy, both in theory and in practice, is incapable of resolving the major economic dilemmas of our time — poverty, environmental degeneration, and unemployment. We shall suggest that these dilemmas call for a new economic agenda. We shall then explore the prospects of locating a genuine resolution to these problems, a resolution that lies beyond the grasp of today's commonly accepted solutions. And this process will lead us to recommend, at the book's conclusion, a twelve-step program for economic recovery.

This book arises out of a specific observation. In our experience the large majority of our economist colleagues and politicians defend the conviction that, if we restore growth in industrial production, then we shall solve several of the distressing problems plaguing today's national and international economy. More precisely, they argue that a restoration of industrial production growth will remedy poverty, environmental degeneration, and unemployment. In our view, however, this conviction is thoroughly simplistic. We have no expectation that a recovery of economic growth in the industrialized nations, either short- or long-term, will alleviate poverty, environmental degeneration, unemployment, and losses in the quality of work. Instead, we believe that we must confront the startling irony that, like a virus that has developed a resistance or immunity to the cure, or like a pest that has developed a defense against the pesticide, these economic malaises have now become immune to the remedy of increased production

1

growth. Ought we not at least to entertain the possibility that these dilemmas now stubbornly and successfully *resist* the solution of increased economic expansion? Ought we not even to consider the possibility that their rigidity has increased precisely in proportion to our efforts to solve them using today's accepted economic instruments? Ought we not, in other words, to entertain the prospect that these economic dilemmas have now become *structural?*

Six Paradoxes

Consider, by way of beginning, several new, bewildering, and seemingly inexplicable developments unfolding in today's economy. At least six paradoxes have surfaced at the heart of the industrialized nations.

The Scarcity Paradox

Our society, a society of unprecedented wealth, experiences unprecedented scarcity.

How is it that a society of enormous wealth also experiences enormous scarcity? Economically we would expect that as material prosperity increased we would have *reduced* scarcity rather than raised it. However, even as economic growth continues and the standard of living rises, a new, generalized feeling of scarcity has permeated our society. Though average incomes are substantially higher than they were twenty-five years ago, the sense in our society that we do not have all that we need is markedly more intense than before. Moreover, we can no longer ignore reports in the press stating that businesses, nonprofit organizations, and governments have had to slash essential expenditures and services. How is it that these reports appear much more frequently now than they did twenty-five years ago, when the average income was *half* of what it is today?

Perhaps the most blatant signal of escalating scarcity at the center of unprecedented wealth is the skyrocketing government deficits of the West. Why do deficits soar seemingly out of control in the wealthy nations, even under governments "committed" to deficit reduction?

The Poverty Paradox

Poverty is rising sharply in the midst of wealthy societies.

Poverty is increasing at an alarming rate precisely at the heart of *wealthy* societies. Again, economically we would expect that the creation of wealth would serve to alleviate poverty. Yet consider the pattern in the industrialized nations, beginning in North America. The United States Federal Bureau of Statistics reports that in 1991 alone over two million more Americans found themselves in poverty than in 1990, bringing the total figure to 35.7 million people, or to 14.2 percent of the American population. This is the highest figure in ten years. According to the Department of Housing and Urban Development, the number of people living in shelters grew by 155 percent between 1984 and 1988, years that belonged to the longest peacetime period of sustained growth in the gross national product in United States' history.[1] Presently even the lowest of the wide-ranging figures estimating the number of homeless people in the United States suggests that more people are homeless than at any time since the Great Depression.[2] Between 1979 and 1989, the rate of child poverty increased by 21 percent in the United States, while the gross national product increased by more than 25 percent.[3] Further, poverty is encroaching upon rural North America, even in the midst of astonishing levels of agricultural production.

Similarly, in Canada poverty increased from 14.2 percent of the population in 1980 to 16 percent in 1992, despite the substantial economic growth of the 1980s.[4] Likewise, though the 1992 United Nations *Human Development Report* ranked Canada the best place in the world to live, child poverty in Canada shot up from 14.5 percent in 1989 to an astounding 18.3 percent in 1991.[5] Currently, in the midst

1. Bread for the World Institute on Hunger and Development, *Hunger 1993: Uprooted People* (Washington, D.C., 1992), 107.
2. Ibid.
3. Ibid., 154. These figures come from the United States Department of Commerce.
4. The Laidlaw Foundation, "Canada and Its Children," *Children and Their Prospects* 1 (Fall 1993): 11.
5. Citizens for Public Justice, "Getting Our House in Order" (Toronto, 1993), 5.

3

of significant wealth, Canada has the second highest level of child poverty in the Western world.[6]

The same paradox afflicts Europe. According to estimates, approximately 50 million people in the European Community live in relative poverty. Reliable statistics estimating the number of poor people in Eastern Europe do not exist, but by all accounts the situation there is even more bleak.

How is it also that, despite the development assistance and relief efforts undertaken by the wealthy nations over several decades, poverty and hunger have substantially *increased* in Africa and other parts of the world?

The Care Paradox

In the midst of more wealth, we have fewer opportunities to practice care than before.

Even as our standard of living rises, opportunities for carrying out those activities that belong to the "sustenance" or "preservation" side of society are continually decreasing. These activities include caring for people in hospitals and schools, for the elderly, for the emotionally distressed, for the condition of soil and water, and for the development of art and culture. Again, economically we would expect that more wealth would generate additional funds for such care activities and would free up the time that people need to practice care. Instead, however, the *reverse* has happened: in the midst of rising prosperity, opportunities for demonstrating care, both financially and personally, have decreased. How is this possible?

The Labor Paradox

Our society's need for more labor is becoming critical even as unemployment rises.

Despite the fact that our society urgently requires additional labor, unemployment continually rises. Perhaps never in the recent past has

6. The Laidlaw Foundation, "Canada and Its Children," 1.

4

our society needed a greater input of labor. The tasks of rebuilding cities, exercising care for people in need, and rehabilitating impaired ecosystems demand a significant amount of labor, and increasingly so. Why is it, then, that even in the midst of economic growth, unemployment, instead of dropping, seems to rise?

The Health Paradox

Even though our level of health care has increased, our level of disease is rising.

Despite stunning achievements and more extensive efforts in health care, the level of disease and illness in our society is escalating. Not long ago Canada's Laboratory Centre for Disease Control declared that science has failed the battle against cancer, for example. Despite the $1.6 billion spent each year by the National Cancer Institute in the United States, cancer mortality rates are rising, while according to the American Cancer Society's 1992 *Cancer Facts and Figures* booklet, "the chances of an American getting cancer during his or her lifetime are one in three."[7] Health care costs have reached a crisis state. Economically we would expect that a society boasting a rising standard of living would have raised rather than lowered its level of health. How is it, then, that the *opposite* appears to be happening?

The Time Paradox

Despite substantially more wealth, we have less and less time in our lives.

In the midst of wealth, we have less and less time on our hands, and we find our daily activities more harried than ever before. Again, economically we would expect that increased wealth would give us more time, not less. In the early 1970s experts predicted that, largely because of automation, the critical social problem of the 1980s and 1990s would be the possession of too much leisure time. In fact,

7. As reported in *Alternatives: Perspectives on Society and Development* 20, 1 (November/December 1993): 3.

however, despite our much higher incomes, we now have far *less* time for nonwork activities than we did in the 1970s. In her recent book *The Overworked American,* Harvard professor Juliet Schor concludes that in the past twenty years working hours have gone up by the equivalent of one month per year.[8]

Three Economic Impasses

These remarkable economic paradoxes are reflections of the new, paradoxical nature that the dilemmas of poverty, environmental degeneration, and unemployment have acquired today. These dilemmas have acquired a new and perplexing element: their apparent resistance, even worsening, in the face of the efforts undertaken in the industrialized nations to solve them.

In Chapter 1 we shall attempt to trace this development. We shall briefly sketch the development of poverty, environmental degeneration, and unemployment over the last several decades, tracking each from the vantage point of the success or failure of the solutions used by the industrialized nations to resolve it — solutions rooted largely in the much vaunted solution of a growth in industrial production. We shall then add a section on the economic ramifications of the changing nature of international conflict after the collapse of the Iron Curtain. Together, these will serve as the backdrop for the discussion of economic renewal that will occupy us throughout the remainder of the book.

Poverty

At the beginning of the 1950s the first articles appeared about what we would later call "development." In 1948 United States President Harry Truman sounded the political alarm for the world as a whole, when in Point 4 of his inaugural address he outlined the West's responsibility with respect to poverty. Globally speaking, Truman and others believed that the extensive transfer of capital — for example, in the form of loans with a term of twenty-five to thirty years — could

8. Juliet Schor, *The Overworked American: The Unexpected Decline of Leisure* (New York: Basic Books, 1991).

remedy poverty. In addition to earmarking scarce production factors, Truman urged the West to earmark capital for the expansion of technological expertise in the Third World. He argued that the West had to set the economic machinery of the developing nations in motion by a "Big Push," the first priority of which was to be the creation of an economic and social infrastructure.

Enthusiastic discussion and activity then began over the planning and programming of the entire process, especially in the context of the United Nations. Soon, however, those working on the issue discovered that much more was involved in the developing countries than a simple economic problem, much more than even the preeminent economic problem, scarcity. It appeared that vigorous cooperation was needed if poverty was to be alleviated — cooperation among those in the various scientific disciplines, politicians, and especially those directly involved, namely the poor.

But clearly, by the beginning of the 1950s (or actually at the acceptance of the Charter of Human Rights in 1948) the industrialized West had opened up visions of a new period for the people of the developing countries. They heard talk of "rising expectations" and of the "Prosperity of the World as a Mutual Responsibility."[9]

Let us now step back and assess the success or failure of the "Big Push" to alleviate poverty between 1950 and the present day. At least five main themes emerge out of this turbulent period of over forty years.

Rising Production, Falling Income First, the period as a whole saw a significant growth in production in the developing countries, averaging 3.3 percent per capita in the 1960s and 2.4 percent in the 1970s. Production increased both in agriculture and in the various industrial sectors. After 1980, however, the *income* trend associated with production growth changed. Taking the developing countries together as a whole, after 1980 income per capita has scarcely grown (0.1%). In several regions of the world, in spite of higher production levels, income per capita has actually dropped. The 1992 *World Development Report* of the World Bank reports that income dropped each year between 1980 and 1990 an average of .9 percent in sub-Saharan Africa, 2.5 percent in the Middle East and northern Africa, and .5 percent in Latin America

9. The title of an address that Queen Juliana of the Netherlands delivered in 1955.

and the Caribbean.[10] This was a repercussion of the recession of the late 1970s, which for many Third World countries meant a substantial drop in their export prices — between 30 and 50 percent.

The end of the eighties and the beginning of the nineties have witnessed an increase in production in parts of the Third World, particularly in Asia, and to a lesser degree in Latin America. A comparable increase has not occurred in Africa. At the same time, a recovery of export prices does not appear to lie on the horizon.

Rising Numbers of Poor People The World Bank estimates that the total number of poor people in the developing countries has increased *without any interruption* between 1950 and the present day.

By 1990, the poor in the Third World numbered 1.1 billion people, an increase of .1 billion from 1985.[11] The expectation is that this figure will continue to rise. "Poverty" here means living at or below the poverty line, which is generally defined using the criterion of the World Health Organization: when one is too poor to obtain a "calorie-adequate diet," then one falls below the poverty line.

Subsisting below the poverty line has horrific consequences for children. UNICEF has estimated that 40,000 children die each day — about 17 million children per year — from lack of necessities and from exhaustion. A further aspect of this horror is that inadequate and inferior nutrition in the first year of life has serious consequences for the development of the brain. The Bread for the World Institute on Hunger and Development's *Hunger 1992* report observes that "one third of all children under the age of 5 in developing countries, or 177 million in all, are so poorly nourished that their development is permanently impaired."[12] One can easily surmise the consequences. The continent of Africa, particularly the countries south of the Sahara, has received the most media attention. But sometimes even where production has *increased* significantly, the number of poor people, in the sense of absolute poverty, has *also* increased significantly. Perhaps the most well known example is Brazil. Though it ranks as the world's fourth largest exporter of foodstuffs, Brazil languishes under the

10. World Bank, *World Development Report 1992: Development and the Environment* (Oxford: Oxford University Press, 1991), 32.

11. World Bank, *World Development Report 1992,* 30.

12. Bread for the World Institute on Hunger and Development, *Hunger 1992: Second Annual Report on the State of World Hunger* (Washington, D.C., 1991), 7.

world's sixth highest malnutrition rate.[13] Despite significant production increases in Brazil, "today seven out of every ten Brazilians lack employment, fair pay and access to land to give them the diet defined as a minimum nutrition."[14]

Widening Income Gaps Thirdly, in most developing countries production growth has not benefited all inhabitants: by and large, the rich have become richer and the poor have become poorer. In other words, the picture of the world as a *whole* — widening income differentials between countries — is now also becoming the picture of the bloc of developing countries itself.

As a result, important differentiations have cropped up within the developing countries. These have led to all sorts of categories of nations, such as the "Newly Industrializing Nations" and the bloc of the world's poorest nations — nations with extremely low income (averaging one-fiftieth of the income of the Group of Seven nations). Not only are the incomes of the inhabitants of the world's poorest nations exorbitantly low, but they continually decrease in absolute terms, and the number of poor people living there escalates.

The period of the past forty years also marks the beginning of a distinction between the relatively poor and the absolutely poor in the Third World. In certain countries the income of one group of people has risen dramatically, while the income of a second group has risen much less dramatically, if at all. This has aroused anger and political tension. Over the last four decades this gap has widened on a large scale in the developing countries, bringing with it the accompanying realities of political repression and human rights violations. Tragically, countries in Asia, Africa, and Latin America have provided legions of examples.

In reality, in only a limited number of cases has an improved economic situation led to better income for all over the last forty years. Examples include South Korea, Taiwan, Singapore, and Malasia. The nature of the industrial production in these and similar countries is striking. In these countries women do the bulk of the factory work. Assembly industries, which are prevalent in these countries, require

13. Jan H. Boer, ed., *The Church and External Debt* (Jos, Nigeria: Institute of Church and Society, 1992), 93.
14. Ibid.

long working hours and low wages. If these industries are to continue operating in the developing countries, then they will do so utilizing fewer and fewer workers, because automation and untenable working conditions will drive workers out of the workplace. In general, the increase in production in such countries has been coupled with forms of social disintegration, which becomes more acute as industries relocate.

Despite the increased economic differentiation among developing countries, as a bloc they have remained close together at international conferences. Thus speculations that a number of the Newly Industrializing Nations would gradually add themselves to the Western nations appear to have been rather premature.

Finally, income differentials across the world as a *whole* have widened sharply over the past three decades. According to the United Nations Development Program's *Human Development Report 1992,* "In 1960 the richest 20% of the world's population had incomes 30 times greater than the poorest 20 percent. By 1990, the richest 20% were getting 60 times more."[15] Similarly, the poorest 20 percent of the world's population receives only .2 percent of global commercial bank lending, 1.3 percent of global investment, 1 percent of global trade, and 1.4 percent of global income.[16] And a statement by the United States Senate Committee on the Budget roughly typifies a scenario happening around the world: "At the start of the 1980s, a Chief Executive Officer made about 29 times as much as the average worker. Today that multiple is close to 100 times."[17]

These figures help to explain the emergence of a new, unexpected development today: the increasing transformation of our society into a "dual" society. The dual nature of our society is reflected in the sudden, astonishing increase in the numbers of uprooted people streaming into the wealthy nations. Uprooted poor people are streaming into the United States from Mexico and other points south and into the European Community from the south and the east. Lech Walesa has eloquently described our society as divided by a curtain no longer made of iron but now of silver. A silver curtain is not as

15. United Nations Development Program, *Human Development Report 1992* (Oxford: Oxford University Press, 1992), 3.
16. Ibid.
17. Quoted in Bread for the World Institute on Hunger and Development, *Hunger 1992,* 162.

thick as iron, and the wealthy nations find themselves in the predicament that it is impossible simply to lock their doors.[18]

Rising Debt Fourthly, the rise in poverty is linked to the shocking burden of debt carried by many countries in the South. The scope of their debt burden has become so enormous that since 1982 the developing countries as a whole have paid more interest and principal to the wealthy countries and their banks than the total amount they received back from them in the form of investments, credits, and development assistance! According to the 1992 *Human Development Report,* "The current debt-related net transfer from the developing to the industrialized countries stands at $50 billion a year."[19] In other words, since 1982 the rising standard of living of the wealthy countries has been partially subsidized by the developing countries.

To grasp the extent to which the debt burden has interfered with the economies of the poor nations, let us explore Third World indebtedness for a moment. In 1990 the total external debt of the developing countries reached $1.35 trillion U.S. Since then the overall figure has scarcely changed, though Africa's debt is still on the rise. But let us attempt to put the figure of $1.35 trillion into perspective. It means that every inhabitant of the North holds a claim of about $1,110 U.S. on the countries of the South. It also means that each year every inhabitant of the North receives between $150 and $200 in interest payments from the South.[20] Conversely, the debt of the poorest developing countries stands at about $81 billion U.S., which means that per capita each inhabitant living there owes approximately $176 to the wealthy nations and their banks and institutions. But the gross national product in these countries stands at no more than $237 per capita per year! This leads to the astonishing conclusion that each inhabitant of these countries must work nine months of his or her life simply to pay off external debt. And every child in these countries, through no action of his or her own, is born into an astonishing debt obligation.

This paints a static picture of Third World debt. But it is in the

---

18. The Bread for the World Institute on Hunger and Development considered the issue of uprooted people so critical that it devoted its entire *Hunger 1993* report to it.

19. United Nations Development Program, *Human Development Report 1992,* 11.

20. This calculation is based on the real interest rate that was effectively paid during the 1980s, namely 17 percent.

11

dynamics of debt that the intractable, horrific reality of poverty in the Third World reveals itself. Four "laws" govern the dynamics of debt today. They make clear that the rising affluence of the wealthy nations is inextricably linked to the increasing impoverishment of the poor.

The first law is that the poor nations must bear the full brunt of external shocks in the world economy, shocks over which they have no control. It is no secret that only the rich nations have access to the creation of so-called key currencies, or currencies that are acceptable in the international exchange. This means that in response to outside shocks, such as an imposition of higher export barriers or a raising of import prices (especially the price of oil!), the poor nations have had no alternative but to borrow money acceptable in the international exchange from foreign banks, simply to remain in position.[21] To gauge the impact of these external shocks over the past decade, note that according to the 1992 *Human Development Report,* "20 of 24 industrial countries now are more protectionist than they were ten years ago . . . [a reality which costs] the developing countries 10 times what they receive in foreign assistance."[22]

The second law is that debts increase *despite* every significant effort on the part of the poor nations to pay them off. This has occurred on a large scale. For example, between 1982 and 1988 the total debt of the Third World more than doubled, despite the fact that together during that same period the Third World nations paid no less than $830 billion to their creditors — an amount more than what they had owed in 1982! Similarly, in 1982 the low income countries of Africa had an official debt of $17 billion, against which they paid $5 billion by 1986. Yet during that same four-year period their debt *doubled* to $34 billion.[23]

How do we explain this startling reality? It occurred because of shockingly high rates of interest in the 1980s: the "developing countries effectively paid an average real interest rate of 17% during the 1980s, compared with 4% by the industrial nations."[24]

The third law is that debts rise *because* of the poor nations' efforts

21. See Michael Moffit, *The World's Money: International Banking from Bretton Woods to the Brink of Insolvency* (New York: Simon and Schuster, 1983).

22. United Nations Development Program, *Human Development Report 1992,* 6-7.

23. For further details see Percy Mistry, *African Debt Revisited: Procrastination or Progress? Forum on Debt and Development* (The Hague, 1991).

24. Cited in United Nations Development Program, *Human Development Report 1992,* 4.

to pay off their debts. This law, known as the law of Irving Fischer ("the more people pay, the more they owe") has also operated on a large and devastating scale.[25] The worldwide economic depression that began in 1979 caused a decline in global demand for products from the Third World. Many poor nations, wanting to get out of the debt trap (especially because of rising interest rates), sought to increase their exports even more, because only increased exports could bring in the key currencies needed to pay off their debts. But in the declining world market, every increase in the quantity of exported goods caused prices to plummet. As a result, export revenues *fell* instead of *rose,* and less money was available to pay off debts *because* of more production. Because of their efforts to pay, the poor nations' indebtedness to the wealthy nations grew.

For the Third World, the combined effect of these three laws has led to the fourth law, that impoverishment rises while debt is being paid off. In the face of the inability to pay escalating debts, creditors have required the poor nations to structurally adjust their economies. The effects of "structural adjustment programs" have sometimes been catastrophic.[26] Frequently they entail lowering wages and decreasing by as much as one-third expenditures in so-called soft, nonexport-related areas, such as health and education. Since 1990 the debt burden has required African countries south of the Sahara to reduce by one-third their expenditures on health and education.[27] Often, such as in Brazil and the Philippines, structural adjustment programs require the promotion of large-scale, export-oriented agriculture at the expense of local culture and appropriate-scale farming, farming that feeds the local population. This transforms small farmers into environmental refugees who have no place to live and no ability to feed their children.[28] The combination of lower wages, sharply decreased levels of health care and education,

25. Ibid., 52.
26. See Susan George, *A Fate Worse Than Debt* (New York: Penguin Books, 1988), part II.
27. In the same vein, Brazil and Mexico have had to cut health budgets to 25 percent of their 1972 levels (Jan H. Boer, ed., *The Church and External Debt,* 95).
28. Jodi Jacobson, a leading expert in the field, estimates the total number of environmental refugees in the world today to be more than 10 million people (in her contribution to Bread for the World Institute on Hunger and Development, *Hunger 1993,* 66).

and the loss of access to land has led to further horrific, grinding, relentless poverty in the Third World.[29]

Indeed, the picture does not appear to be brightening. Before 1990, the World Bank calculated that the African nations' "debt servicing," or paying the interest and principal of their loans, would require annually about 5 percent of the entire income of the African countries. Calculate in a population increase of at least 3 percent, and the actual scope of the problem begins to become clear. For these figures mean that if production grows by more than 8 percent per year, then the average income per capita in Africa will not *decrease*. But of course economic growth of 8 percent per year is out of the question for these countries. As a result, in the words of Robert McNamara, spoken in April 1990, "The situation five years from now is likely to be worse, not better." Infant mortality is again on the increase in Africa, and Africa faces "the dismal prospect that [it] may enter the twenty-first century with a greater proportion of [its] population non-literate and unskilled than it did at the beginning of the 1960s."[30]

Falling Expectations   These realities have not gone unnoticed. In fact, the expectations of those in the Third World had risen substantially with the ratification of the Charter of Economic Rights and Duties of States (1989) and with the vision articulated in "Toward a Better International Economic Order" (1976), drafted at a special session of the United Nations. Based on these agreements, people sensed that political leaders would seek, however falteringly, to drive back world poverty. These documents sought to define the contours of an economy that would clarify the mutual responsibility of private institutions, national governments, and international bodies. They also sought to foster an international recognition that the ideology of the "invisible hand," which has caused such human suffering and injustice, has sent both us and our international economic structures down the wrong track.

29. In the case of the Philippines, this of course does not tell the whole story. The average life expectancy in the Philippines has improved by ten years during the last three decades, and the adult literacy rate grew to 92 percent of the population. However, these averages may never be used to justify the misery and poverty that virtually destroy the poorest segments of the population and that, to a large degree, are the direct consequence of the extremely high debt owed to foreign creditors.

30. *Maseru Declaration on the Debt Crisis as It Affects Human Rights,* reprinted in Jan H. Boer, ed., *The Church and External Debt,* 207.

Expectations fell considerably, however, for at least two reasons. It is instructive to consider these reasons. First, in the developing countries, political liberation did not lead to the establishment of a new and unique relationship with the structure of the economy. It rapidly became clear that the pattern of economic relations, both within and between countries, was not easy to alter. In 1985, during a trip to the West, President Nyerere of Tanzania stated that Western governments repeatedly tell the political leaders of Third World countries that they have made mistakes. Unquestionably, said Nyerere, they have. But he added:

> Poverty and underdevelopment in Africa cannot be seen separately from the wealth and technological "headstart" present elsewhere. The existing pattern of the division of wealth in the world is a legacy which buckles over independent Africa. But it is not Africa's own doing. It is not insignificant that one quarter of the world's population receives four-fifths of the world's income. Wealth creates more wealth, and poverty leads to more poverty, as a result of increased investment possibilities and one's power or powerlessness in relation to others.

As for mistakes made by political leaders in the developing countries themselves, we believe that in numerous situations, driven by self-aggrandizement, they have shown little or no interest in the *poor* of their countries.

Secondly, the development dialogue has produced a series of far-reaching ideas and well-formulated proposals.[31] Nonetheless, lacking the political will to act constructively, the governments of the West have never taken seriously the vast majority of these suggestions. Politicians have been able to move on effortlessly to other agendas, partly because public interest in poverty has not been strong. Sadly, in our assessment a misplaced optimism, driven by the faith that rising production and the rising incomes that accompany it will automatically trickle down to all of the people of the world, especially to those in the poor regions, has weakened the resolve to implement funda-

31. Consider, for example, the Willy Brandt reports *North-South: A Programme for Survival* (Cambridge, Mass.: MIT Press, 1980) and *Common Crisis North-South: Cooperation for World Recovery* (Cambridge, Mass.: MIT Press, 1983).

mental reform. Our understanding of economic processes and of the events of the past forty years does not support this optimism. In and of itself, rising production does not lead to just distribution: just distribution requires the empowerment of the less endowed and an embrace of justice by the privileged.

In this context, if we consider poverty not just a human problem but also a matter of justice among nations, then the failure of the wealthy nations to live up to the promises they made in 1968 is genuinely disturbing. In 1968, at the General Assembly of the United Nations, the wealthy nations committed themselves to earmarking .7 percent of their gross national product for financial assistance to the developing countries. In fact, however, only the Scandinavian countries and the Netherlands have lived up to this promise. While those countries' contributions have exceeded .7 percent, Canada, the United States, Great Britain, and Japan have fallen far short. To put this failure in perspective for a moment, consider that Maurice Strong, in an address entitled "Beyond Rio: A New Role for Canada," suggests that if the industrialized nations simply live up to their original .7 percent commitment, then they will have freed up enough funds largely to meet the objectives of Agenda 21 (the political agreement drafted at the Earth Summit in Rio de Janeiro in 1992), especially the primary goal of eradicating poverty.[32]

Poverty also poses an enormous challenge to nongovernment organizations, including the churches, a challenge exacerbated by the failure of the nations.

*   *   *

Faced with these baffling realities — declining income in the developing countries, despite production growth; the uninterrupted increase in the number of poor people in the developing countries since 1950; widening income gaps on a startling scale, together with the sudden, unexpected streams of uprooted people around the world; the massive subsidization of the North by the South since 1982; the impossible debt burden of the developing countries; and falling expectations — ought we not to conclude that the *form* that the North has given to

32. Maurice Strong, "Beyond Rio: A New Role for Canada," O. D. Skelton Memorial Lecture (Ottawa: External Affairs and International Trade Canada), 11-12. The address was delivered in Vancouver on November 10, 1992.

its responsibility to alleviate poverty is fundamentally defective? Indeed, it appears that our solutions either have not helped or have dramatically worsened the problems. How else are we to explain the perplexing fact that even such distinguished international institutions as the International Monetary Fund (IMF) and the World Bank now find themselves engaged in substantial negative net transfers of money? The 1992 *Human Development Report* states that "between 1983 and 1987 net IMF transfers to developing countries turned from plus $7.6 billion to minus $7.9 billion" (with an annual average between 1986 and 1990 of $6.3 billion), while "in 1991 new World Bank transfers were minus $1.7 billion."[33] These reverse transfers led the report to conclude that "the Bretton Woods Institutions . . . failed many developing countries at their time of greatest need."[34]

Moreover, how else are we to understand the reality that *every day* an amount of money roughly equivalent to the total debt of the developing countries circulates uncontrollably in the "pure" financial sphere — an amount *thirty to forty times* more than that which circulates in the "direct" sphere of buying and selling goods and services? These uncoordinated capital movements threaten the international monetary system itself, as we saw in 1992 when Great Britain and France were forced to defend their currencies by taking them out of the European Monetary Union.

Poverty and the failure of the solutions emanating from the "Big Push" therefore form our first indication that our economy must be fundamentally renewed. We must confront the baffling conclusion that, in spite of increased economic expertise and the vast expansion of technologies available for fighting poverty, the main task is now larger than it was even ten years ago. This daunting reality makes it incumbent upon us to locate and develop an answer within our economic order itself to the seeming intractability of poverty. The fact that *people* have created the present situation means that we must search much more seriously and diligently for the deeper-lying causes of poverty. And we must suggest what kind of renewal and reform are required if we are to pull back from a global economic system that has led us to the edge of an abyss.

33. United Nations Development Program, *Human Development Report 1992*, 51.

34. Ibid.

The Environment

Discussions about the environment began with *The Limits to Growth,* the first Report of the Club of Rome, released in early 1972.[35] Since then, an enormous amount of material and data addressing environmental issues has been published.

The environmental degeneration flagged in *The Limits to Growth* has since become a reality in many areas of the world. At the same time, many people have begun to recognize that, because clean air, pure water, fertile soil, and sufficient quiet are essential to human life, environmental issues form a critical problem within economic life itself. More and more we hear environmental realities described as "new scarcities," for example. In 1992 the United Nations Conference on Environment and Development in Brazil (UNCED, or the Earth Summit), facilitated by Maurice Strong, addressed environmental issues in a more far-reaching fashion than the Stockholm Conference had twenty years earlier. Recognizing that in many respects poverty is both a cause and an effect of environmental degradation, UNCED also linked the need to remediate environmental damage with the need to battle poverty.

These developments notwithstanding, over the last twenty years the environment itself has dramatically deteriorated. Environmental degradation is a bitter reality today. The assault on creation proceeds on a grand scale, despite government legislation, individual efforts, the activities of nongovernment organizations, and certain efforts within the business and scientific communities.

In Chapter 6 we shall explore the extent to which Agenda 21, the political agreement drafted at the UNCED conference in Brazil, provides a genuine agenda for addressing the new economic and environmental realities.[36] At this stage, we shall supply a brief sketch of contemporary environmental realities.

The Ozone Layer   The depletion of the ozone layer forms perhaps the most serious environmental threat to the lives of people, animals, and

35. Dennis Meadows et al., *The Limits to Growth* (New York: New American Library, 1972).
36. Nicholas A. Robinson, ed., *Agenda 21 and the UNCED Proceedings* (New York: Oceana Publications Ltd., 1992).

plants. According to the World Resource Institute's 1993 *Environmental Almanac,* "In the last decade, ozone depletion has overtaken smog and acid rain and has gone to the top of the list of human insults to Earth's atmosphere."[37] Twenty years ago researchers recognized that the thinning of the ozone layer, largely through the emission of chlorofluorocarbons (CFCs) used in the production of a wide range of household and other products, would dramatically increase rates of skin cancer and cataracts. They now also know, thanks to studies from Australia, where the effects of ozone depletion are most advanced, that a thinner ozone shield damages crops, harms delicate food chains, and diminishes the durability of outdoor materials.[38]

Despite this knowledge, some twenty million tons of CFCs have been released into the atmosphere. The United States National Aeronautics and Space Administration (NASA) reports that "The earth's protective ozone concentration has decreased an average of about 20 percent over the past twenty years, largely as a result of interaction with CFC's."[39] Skin cancers have increased dramatically in the United States over the past two decades, with over 400,000 new cases diagnosed each year.[40] The United Nations Environment Program (UNEP) estimates that an expected 10 percent ozone loss over a region covering much of Canada, the United States, and Europe will cause a 26 percent increase in nonmelanoma skin cancers and will generate 1.6 million new cataract cases.[41]

After years of opposition by industry, often in the form of minimizing the dangers, in 1987 forty-four countries signed the landmark Montreal Protocol on Substances That Deplete the Ozone Layer. The signatories agreed to reduce CFC production by 50 percent by the year 2000. Since then many countries have vigorously pursued reductions in the production of CFCs and have even independently stepped up their commitments. Germany, for example, will ban CFC production after 1994, and Canada and the United States have agreed to phase out CFC production by 1996. The need for these actions be-

37. World Resources Institute, *The 1993 Information Please Environmental Almanac* (New York: Houghton Mifflin Company, 1993), 303.

38. Ibid.

39. Taken from Marc Lappé, *Chemical Deception: The Toxic Threat to Health and the Environment* (San Francisco: Sierra Club Books, 1991), 51.

40. Ibid., 52.

41. Ibid., 308.

came much more acute when Mount Pinatubo erupted in the Philippines in 1991, spewing out an estimated 20 million tons of sulfate aerosol, another ozone-damaging particle.

From the start, however, experts have maintained that only an *immediate* 90 to 95 percent reduction of CFC emissions will be sufficient to salvage the ozone layer, because the "lag effect" of ozone-damaging chemicals will mean ongoing ozone damage well into the twenty-first century.

Meanwhile, the signatories have revisited the Montreal Protocol and have formally agreed to ban CFC production worldwide by the year 2000. It remains to be seen, however, whether this injunction will be followed everywhere around the world. To make compliance in the Third World feasible, on January 1, 1991, the Multilateral Ozone Fund was established to help finance the transfer of new technologies to the Third World.

Global Warming The Intergovernmental Panel on Climate Change (IPCC), a panel of scientists operating under the auspices of the United Nations, estimates that a doubling of atmospheric carbon dioxide concentrations from preindustrial levels would lead to an increase of the average global annual surface temperature by 1.5 to 4.5 degrees Celsius. Changes in average global temperature of this magnitude have never before occurred in human history.

These projections have generated considerable alarm. Many experts predict that global warming will raise sea levels to such an extent that massive flooding and coastal destruction will occur. They also predict that ecosystems will be unable to adapt, that tropical storms will become more frequent and severe, and that rainfall patterns will alter dramatically. The United States Environmental Protection Agency (EPA) has also identified global warming as the primary environmental cause for concern for human health.[42]

Meanwhile, at the Earth Summit in Brazil, 153 nations signed the United Nations Framework Convention on Climate Change. However, "the treaty does not set binding targets or require specific actions — largely at the insistence of the United States."[43] Further, many critics

42. Ibid., 49.
43. World Resources Institute, *The 1993 Information Please Environmental Almanac,* 313.

believe that the treaty's stipulations are far too meager: "It calls for —
but does not require — stabilizing emissions of greenhouse gases [such
as carbon dioxide and CFCs] at 1990 levels in the industrialized countries by the end of the century."[44] Because, according to an IPCC
estimate, stabilization of concentrations of greenhouse gases in the
atmosphere will require a 60 percent reduction in their emissions, the
amount of greenhouse gases in the atmosphere will likely rise.

It is significant that 75 percent of all emissions of carbon dioxide
(CO_2), the principal greenhouse gas, originates in the industrialized
nations. The United States is the world leader in CO_2 emissions, both
in total output and on a per capita basis. Annually the United States
generates over five billion tons of CO_2 emissions, or twenty-two tons
per inhabitant of the United States.[45] Canada, the former Soviet
Union, China, Japan, Germany, and several other countries also contribute substantially. What remains entirely unclear is how even a small
decrease in CO_2 emissions can occur in practice. Levels of CO_2
emissions are closely linked to both energy consumption and transportation patterns, especially the use of automobiles and trucks. Electric utilities, for example, account for one-third of all CO_2 emissions
in the United States, while the transportation sector accounts for
another one-third.

A number of studies have documented the rising dependence
on the car in North America. The United States alone boasts 190
million cars, and the number of miles traveled in the United States
has doubled since 1970, largely offsetting whatever automobile pollution control gains have been made.[46] Studies have also shown that
damage created by the car extends well beyond CO_2 emissions. When,
in addition to smog and local environmental threats, one considers
traffic accidents and fatalities, noise pollution, congestion, and loss of
land and space, then perhaps indeed "one might reasonably argue that
the car has diminished, rather than enhanced, our quality of life."[47]
The United States Department of Transportation estimates that in
1989 "congestion on interstate highways caused 8 billion hours in
delay and tens of billions of dollars in wasted fuel and productivity.

44. Ibid.
45. Ibid., 319.
46. Ibid., 79-80.
47. Ibid.

By the end of the year 2000 . . . these delays on the nation's highways could increase fourfold."[48] Further, the problems of traffic congestion are much more acute in highly dense urban centers in the Third World, where traffic fatalities are reported to be twenty times higher than in the industrialized world.[49]

Yet fanatic automobile lobbies have continually attempted to minimize such factors, preferring instead to glorify the car as a symbol of freedom and independence.

Protecting the climate will cost huge sums of money (though not protecting it will cost much more), money that the nations of the Third World do not have. The World Environment Fund, established at the end of 1990, is therefore important. This fund, financed by contributions from the industrialized nations, will serve to enhance Third World efforts to protect the world's climate. It thus runs parallel to the CFC fund for protecting the ozone layer.

Acid Rain Attention to air pollution over the past twenty years has focused largely on the problem of acid rain. Sulfur dioxide emissions, the principal cause of acid rain, have declined in the industrialized countries over the past twenty years. Yet the issue remains significant in various regions of the world. The 1993 *Environmental Almanac* reports that "in many cases the use of very tall smokestacks has served simply to transport pollutants to another region downwind."[50] A good deal of acid rain in Canada originates in the United States. Similarly, acid rain falling on the Scandinavian countries has its primary source in England, the former Soviet Union, and Eastern and Western Europe.[51] And 85 percent of the lakes in New Hampshire cannot buffer the effects of acid rain, while half of these lakes carry levels of sulfur dioxide that experts consider too high.

The issues therefore have international dimensions. International conferences draft policy objectives, while the European Parliament entertains the possibility of a "Delta Plan" against acid rain. It is about time: 75 percent of Europe's forests are now experiencing

48. Ibid., 80.
49. Worldwatch Institute, *State of the World 1991* (New York: W. W. Norton & Company, 1991), 58.
50. World Resources Institute, *The 1993 Information Please Environmental Almanac,* 96.
51. Ibid.

damaging levels of sulfur deposits.[52] Estimates suggest that over half of the forests in the Netherlands are no longer thriving. Acid rain has damaged half of Germany's forests, while in Eastern European countries the figure is somewhat higher. Switzerland has begun to take steps against the ongoing destruction of forest areas in the Swiss Alps. In Scandinavian countries air pollution originating elsewhere has poisoned fish in many lakes. Similarly, estimates suggest that four thousand lakes in Sweden are "biologically dead." And acid rain harms not just soil and vegetation, but also buildings, clothing, and health.

Biodiversity The scope of the plunder of nature has also become evident in losses in biological diversity. Reports from the United Nations Environment Program (UNEP) and the Food and Agriculture Organization (FAO) speculate that 30 to 40 percent of all known existing species may become extinct over the next forty years. They surmise that this rapid loss of biological diversity will severely reduce the earth's potential to supply species of medicinal and economic value, as well as genetic material that could help countries adapt to global warming.

The plunder of nature displays itself most spectacularly in the slash and burn of tropical forests and in the mass stripping of ecosystems in oceans and seas. These areas remain largely unprotected. The destruction of rain forests has received considerable media attention, largely because, though they occupy 7 percent of the world's land surface, they contain 50 percent of the world's species. And so severe is overfishing that the government of Canada, in an unprecedented move, has banned cod fishing indefinitely off the coast of Newfoundland and Labrador — an economic lifeline for these regions — in an effort to replenish stocks.

Ought we not, then, to consider the possibility that, if future generations are to have the ability to provide for their needs, and if we are to prevent the ongoing destruction of species, our thinking and action require dramatic change?

Toxic Chemical Waste The scope of chemical contamination throughout the world appears to have exceeded earlier estimates by experts.

52. Worldwatch Institute, *State of the World 1993* (New York: W. W. Norton & Company, 1991), 6.

Recent information detailing the amount of contamination and waste present in Eastern Europe is startling. Soils, surface waters, and groundwaters around the world, including North America, have increasingly become contaminated. According to the United States Environmental Protection Agency's *Toxic Release Inventory,* industry in the United States now releases 20 billion pounds of toxic chemicals annually.[53] Estimates suggest that over the last thirty years 750 million tons of toxic waste from chemical production have been dumped in hazardous waste sites across the United States.[54] While some strides have been taken by chemical producers, it must be said that the overall attitude in the chemical industry is one of nonchalance and that the industry continues to create toxic waste with very little difficulty. Indeed, the United States General Accounting Office reports that current law permits as much as 95 percent of all chemical emissions to go unreported.[55]

The 1984 Union Carbide disaster in Bhopal, India, brought the effects of the chemical industry into broad daylight, if only temporarily. The disaster flushed out many questions. Spurred on by the Bhopal drama — in which approximately 3,500 people died and tens of thousands were disabled, many permanently — researchers have demonstrated that the Third World pays a proportionately higher price, in the form of damage to health and the environment, for chemical production. According to the World Health Organization, each year pesticides in the Third World cause the deaths of approximately twenty thousand people and illness for several hundred thousand people. The Third World is also increasingly becoming a dumping ground for hazardous substances banned in the industrialized nations. In a macabre irony, the United States still produces the banned substance DDT and exports it to the developing countries.

The effects of toxic chemical pollution are also evident in agricultural practices in the industrialized nations. Chemical fertilizer and pesticide runoff leaches into groundwater and rivers to such an extent that it now seriously threatens the quality of drinking water in the developed as well as the developing countries. Approximately 40 per-

53. Barry Commoner, *Making Peace with the Planet* (New York: Pantheon Books, 1990), 31.

54. Marc Lappé, *Chemical Deception,* 37.

55. World Resources Institute, *The 1993 Information Please Environmental Almanac,* 188.

24

cent of all wells in Ontario, for example, contain chemical contaminants, the primary source of which is agriculture.

Agriculture Issues in agriculture, not only in the Third World but also in North America, mirror the dynamics described in this chapter to a striking degree. Along with startling increases in production, the three impasses described in this chapter — poverty, environmental degeneration, and unemployment — are stark realities in agriculture.

Consider that between 1950 and 1987, according to United States government statistics, the total output of crops and livestock in the United States rose by an astonishing 80 percent, while labor input declined by 71 percent and chemical input (insecticides, herbicides, and fungicides) increased by 484 percent.[56] Then juxtapose this with the fact that during this same period, again according to U.S. government statistics, *net farm income dropped by 32 percent.*[57] In the midst of these unprecedented levels of agricultural production, this period also witnessed what one commentator has called "one of the most consequential migrations of history": the migration, both forced and unforced, of literally millions of people from rural communities in Canada and the United States to cities.[58]

The replacement of once-traditional farming practices with large-scale, monocultural, and petrochemically dependent agriculture has had a profound and well-documented impact. Many commentators, among them farmers, agree that the loss of diversification caused by what has now become "orthodox" agriculture has led to the severe disruption not only of delicate ecosystems but also of the rural communities that had attuned themselves to some degree to sustaining them.

Environmentally, "orthodox" agricultural practices have led to soil and water contamination, to erosion on a shocking scale, and to disease. With soils made vulnerable to erosion, soil erosion rates are now higher than in the 1930s' dust bowl.[59] Topsoil losses in Iowa now exceed the amount of grain harvested there fivefold; in the state of Washington, twentyfold.[60] Where Iowa once had an average of

56. Cited in Barry Commoner, *Making Peace with the Planet,* 85-86.
57. Ibid., 86.
58. Wendell Berry, *Home Economics* (San Francisco: North Point Press, 1987), 129.
59. Wendell Berry, *What Are People For?* (San Francisco: North Point Press, 1990), 124.
60. Ibid.

sixteen inches of prime topsoil, it now has eight.[61] Every hour, about eight acres of prime topsoil floats past Memphis, Tennessee, as the Mississippi River permanently carries away millions of tons of soil.[62] Monocultural and aggressive farming practices have also led to losses in genetic diversity, which contributed to minimizing the damage caused by insects prior to the infusion of pesticides.

Levels of agriculturally related disease have also risen dramatically. Though such figures are difficult to establish with certainty, the National Research Council of the National Academy of Sciences estimates that each year twenty thousand additional cases of cancer occur in the United States because "the average consumer is exposed to pesticide residues . . . in nearly every food."[63] Further, cancer rates among farmers exposed to pesticides are markedly higher, sometimes by six to eight times, than in the rest of the population.[64]

To make matters worse, poverty has struck parts of rural communities, poverty perhaps most evident in the crushing debt crisis that afflicts agriculture. Because of dependence on a single crop or livestock, large-scale, petrochemically dependent agriculture leaves increasingly little margin for "error" (such as too little or too much rainfall). Further, because the effectiveness of pesticides diminishes as insects develop defenses against them, more chemical input is required, even as the prices of inputs rise.[65] With increasingly little ability to rebound from or absorb "error" and with higher prices for inputs, farmers have had to borrow often astronomical sums of money over the last several decades. Together, these factors have made them even more vulnerable to wildly fluctuating prices and interest rates, resulting in the need to borrow even more. This in part accounts for grim statistics describing farm foreclosures. Farm poverty in the United States rose from 17.7 percent in 1980 to 25 percent in 1985.[66] Between 1980 and 1988, three hundred thousand

61. Al Gore, *Earth in the Balance* (New York: Houghton Mifflin Company, 1992), 3.

62. Ibid.

63. Barry Commoner, *Making Peace with the Planet,* 51.

64. Cf. ibid.

65. Barry Commoner calculates that between 1950 and 1987 the productivity of agricultural chemicals decreased by 69 percent (*Making Peace with the Planet,* 86).

66. Alternative Women in Development, "Reaganomics and Women: Structural Adjustment U.S. Style: 1980-1992" (Washington, D.C.: Alt-WID, 1990), 12.

family farms disappeared in the United States, and by 1988, 4.9 percent of American farms earned 54.5 percent of total farm profit.[67]

Together, these dynamics have also led to wholesale losses and dislocations in labor, driven in part by a bias against the assumed "drudgery" of farm work.

Large-scale agriculture has often meant even larger-scale dependency, and the slimmer the margins of error the greater the scale of disaster.[68] At the same time, however, the reconnoitering of Wendell Berry and others has shown that sustainable, diversified forms of agriculture and culture do exist, forms that preserve rural ecosystems and communities and that remain relatively immune to the debilitating fluctuations of prices and interest rates. Reliable studies, based on the study of actual farms, have demonstrated that even on a large scale, farming practices that use no chemical fertilizers or pesticides can maintain, relatively speaking, both productivity and sustainability.[69]

Human Health More and more today we read about the damage that chemical substances do to human health. We have described several effects above. But inhabitants of islands in the Pacific Ocean, where France conducted uninterrupted weapons tests until 1992, provide further heartrending examples. The international community remained silent about these tests, though birth defects and chromosome damage have occurred there on a large scale. Even now, France has merely imposed an indefinite "moratorium" on these tests, pending further international security developments.

In the industrialized nations, government regulations have lagged far behind the realities of chemical substance effects on workers and on children. And a recent UNEP report states:

1.2 billion city dwellers world-wide are exposed to excessive levels of sulfur dioxide. Nearly a third of the cities monitored within the

---

67. Ibid., 11.

68. Wendell Berry has said about a specific context, "The introduction of industrial technology . . . involves a gross simplification of the agriculture itself as well as a drastic complication of the economy. It requires a cash economy and credit [and favors] the larger producer" (Wendell Berry, *The Unsettling of America: Culture and Agriculture* [New York: Avon Books, 1977], 178).

69. See Wendell Berry, *The Unsettling of America,* 194, and Barry Commoner, *Making Peace with the Planet,* 97.

Global Environment Monitoring System have levels of nitrogen dioxide that exceed the official guidelines of the World Health Organization and carbon monoxide levels in more than one half of the cities exceed WHO guidelines. Overall, only 20 percent of the world's 2.26 billion urban dwellers live in cities where air quality is acceptable. The health of many of the others is now being directly affected by high levels of airborne pollution.[70]

The 1992 *World Development Report* of the World Bank states that only 2 percent of sewage in Latin America is treated for sanitation.[71] Meanwhile, 1 billion people in the world live without safe water supplies and 1.7 billion without sanitation.[72]

Deforestation Over the past twenty years environmental issues in general have become critical in the Third World. Tragically, in a number of regions the poor must damage the environment in order to survive. The 1987 Brundtland report on sustainable development, *Our Common Future,* provided impetus for a worldwide discussion on the dilemma that in many instances fighting poverty involves wreaking destruction on the environment, a dilemma that in the Third World is utterly real.[73] The ongoing presence of poverty in the Third World preempts a solution to the environmental problem in the Third World.

Deforestation and erosion form perhaps the most critical examples of ecological devastation in the Third World. They are, of course, closely linked. Poverty alone, however, does not create Third World environmental deterioration. United Nations reports note that Asian electrical industries, for example, are the most polluting in the world. The concentration of carbon in the atmosphere over China and East Asia is higher than in the rest of the world.

While deforestation has received considerable attention in recent years, the extra attention has not brought an end to the destruction.

---

70. United Nations Environment Program, *Urban Air Pollution* (New York: United Nations, 1991), Foreword.

71. World Bank, *World Development Report 1992,* 16.

72. Ibid., 171.

73. World Commission on Environment and Development, *Our Common Future* (Oxford: Oxford University Press, 1987).

In 1989 workers cut down or burned trees that covered the equivalent of three and one-half times the surface of Lake Ontario or the state of Vermont. Further, between 1979 and 1989, deforestation increased by 90 percent. According to the calculations of the renowned Norman Myers, Amazon forests will disappear in twenty-eight years if the present pace of devastation continues. Vast destruction is also occurring in the Philippines, Sarawak, India, Thailand, Madagascar, the Ivory Coast, and Zaire.

Deforestation counts rapid erosion, floods, and climate changes among its effects. It also creates deserts, which are increasing at a rate of six million hectares per year around the world. UNEP estimates that 35 percent of the world's land surface is in various stages of desertification.[74] Reforestation programs offer meager help when one juxtaposes them with the scope of the problem they seek to counteract, though reforestation does help to reduce the amount of carbon dioxide in the atmosphere.

According to the 1993 *Environmental Almanac,* "About 25 percent of the carbon dioxide released to the atmosphere comes from carbon released when forests are cleared. Thus, environmentalists worry that further deforestation will contribute to global warming, which in turn may lead to further extinction of many species as temperatures, habitats, and conditions change."[75] Meanwhile, as noted above, the extinction of plant and animal species proceeds at a pace of several species every day. Tropical rain forests provide a reservoir of genetic resources. The demand in the Northern Hemisphere for hardwood and cheap beef, coupled with the exorbitant debts of the Third World countries, significantly influences the current rate and scale of deforestation.

The Law of the Sea Convention Though it was difficult to ratify, by 1987, 159 countries had signed the Law of the Sea Convention, an agreement that gave proper due to the rights of Third World countries. Whether or not the convention will ever be enforced, however, remains a very open question. The Reagan administration put a damper over the entire affair, and as a result several governments in Western

74. Bread for the World Institute on Hunger and Development, *Hunger 1993,* 65.

75. World Resources Institute, *The 1993 Information Please Environmental Almanac,* 328-29.

Europe have hesitated to follow through. The agreement regulates, among other things, the extraction of raw materials from the ocean floor. The United States government, preferring to view the ocean floor as hunting grounds for private corporations, objected to that portion of the convention. As a result, the Reagan administration effectively annulled the Law of the Sea Convention.

Recently, however, the convention became ratified, with 1994 marking the year in which it is to come into effect. Nevertheless, of the sixty countries that have ratified the convention, all but two (Iceland and Malta) are developing countries. Without the participation of a major developed country, the enforcement of the convention remains suspect. Many people in the international community, encouraged by United States Vice President Al Gore's stance on environmental issues, hope that the Clinton administration will revisit the Law of the Sea Convention and ratify it. They are also gratified that the present government of Canada, during Canada's recent federal election campaign, committed itself to ratification.

Energy Supply Many of the problems identified above culminate in the issue of energy supply and its future. In the last forty years the world's population has consumed more energy than in the entire history of the world from its beginning until 1950. Since 1945, energy usage has risen about 5 percent per year, which translates to a doubling of energy consumption every fourteen years. A rising standard of living demands a rising consumption of energy. North America is the largest culprit: together Canadians and Americans consume twice the energy of Central Europeans, and seven to eight times the energy of people living in the developing countries. Meanwhile, in the words of the 1993 *Environmental Almanac,* "The combined production, distribution, and consumption of energy is the greatest single source of stress on the environment. It also poses threats to human health."[76]

The primary sources of energy for household use in the poor countries are wood, manure, and agricultural scraps. While for people in the wealthy part of the world energy is largely a matter of prices (for oil, gas, and electricity), for people in the poor part of the world it is primarily a matter of mounting shortages.

Where, then, will the Third World find energy, if its inhabitants

76. Ibid., 70.

are to move to a higher standard of living than the critically inadequate level they now suffer under? Coal is plentiful in the Third World, but a coal economy has harmful effects on the environment and leads to mountains of rubbish. Discussion over the possibilities of nuclear energy and its application has proceeded unabated, despite the fact that no solution has been found for safely disposing of nuclear waste. Meanwhile, the dumping of radioactive waste in oceans continues.

Since 1979, supplying energy by means of "renewable" energy sources, such as the sun, wind, ocean, biogas, and water, has received more attention. At the moment, these sources account for approximately 20 percent of the world's energy supply. Experts agree that we can use energy much more efficiently than we do now.

*   *   *

A few years ago the Worldwatch Institute predicted that in the future the succumbing of ecosystems will pose more of a threat to global security than national aggression will. We shall not speculate as to which will form the more serious threat. Nevertheless, from the foregoing it is clear that an ongoing and unprecedented assault on ecosystems is occurring today on a worldwide scale.

We can be thankful that some positive steps have been taken over the past twenty years. But how are we to assess the ability of present-day efforts to reverse what United States Vice President Al Gore has rightly called "the growing evidence of an ecological holocaust?"[77] How are we to understand their effectiveness in the light of an eloquent 1988 Christmas address by Queen Beatrix of the Netherlands? She stated, "What we now face is the prospect of the annihilation of the earth not in a single blow but in a silent drama. The earth is slowly dying, and the unthinkable — the end of life itself — is still thinkable." Indeed, it seems clear that we must admit that our present-day solutions, despite the intensity of effort behind them, have not substantially slowed, much less reversed, the rapid rate of environmental destruction. Ought we not to conclude that, *in and of themselves,* present-day efforts — as essential as they are — do not and cannot address the *source* of our environmental malaise?

77. Al Gore, *Earth in the Balance,* 245.

The entire complex of environmental issues — issues that appear to go hand in hand with current production methods and consumption patterns in the industrialized nations — thus forms the second indication that our economy requires fundamental renewal. Evidently our current economic system is not in a position to safeguard the ecological stability that humanity requires. That which is environmentally problematic is also economically problematic.

At the same time, a new economic agenda may never accept solutions to our threatening environmental malaise that impede efforts to alleviate poverty, in both the short and the long term. And as we shall see in a moment, such solutions may also not further debilitate our employment system.

The Employment System

Warnings sound not only from the biosphere but also from the "sociosphere."

Unemployment in the United States stands at about 7.8 percent. In Canada the figure hovers around 11 percent, while in the European Community it stands at 10 percent. Though reliable statistics for Eastern Europe are not available, we may assume that overall they are even higher, and the Third World languishes under widespread unemployment averaging between 30 and 40 percent. To these unemployment figures we must add those people who, for whatever reason, rely on systems other than the unemployment system. We must also add the large number of people who would like a job but whom the government cannot register as looking for work. The actual figures must therefore be substantially higher.

In the industrialized nations of the West, unemployment slowly dropped during the 1980s, only to rebound again at the beginning of the 1990s. The rise in employment during the 1980s ought not to delude us, however. New employment growth has consisted largely of part-time jobs, almost half of which, according to the Economic Council of Canada's report *Good Jobs, Bad Jobs,* are *involuntarily* part-time.[78] The figures also mask another significant development in the

78. Economic Council of Canada, *Good Jobs, Bad Jobs* (Ottawa: Canadian Government Publishing Centre, 1990), 11.

labor market: an astronomical "33 percent of all U.S. workers do not have permanent jobs."[79] These workers represent the fastest growing segment of the labor force. And again and again today we read litanies of massive layoffs and job losses.

Indeed, we appear to be headed toward what already in 1958 Hannah Arendt labeled "a society of laborers without labor."[80] For do not our *production* methods and the technological innovation that they embrace bring with them the steady elimination of employment? The connection between job losses and the structure of production remains concealed as long as economic growth remains strong, as it did during the 1970s. During the 1980s, however, the linkage came into broad daylight. For as we shall describe later, when the percentage of growth in *productivity* surpasses the percentage of growth in the *gross national product,* as it did in the 1980s, then a loss of jobs occurs. Industrialized societies therefore find themselves in a new dilemma, namely, that if they wish simply to maintain present employment levels, then they must pursue vigorous, uninterrupted growth in the gross national product at all costs. And is this what we really want? Is it even possible?

The debate about employment has been advanced by research that shows that for most of the working population the quality of work has markedly deteriorated. This makes the issue of work satisfaction much more acute. A Dutch economist, L. U. De Sitter, has attempted to explain this deterioration with a "polarization hypothesis": "This means that a direction develops within the labor market structure whereby both lower and higher qualified tasks increase in relative terms, but the tasks of the broad middle group decrease."[81] De Sitter's view of the role of automation in employment is also important: "Automation either begins or strengthens a development whereby a division of labor creates a few qualitatively complex tasks but a relatively larger number of routine or menial tasks. Clear drops in the level of the meaning and quality of work occur in the larger *middle* group of qualified workers, such as qualified office employees (that is, trained and independent workers who are not part of management)."[82] In a similar vein, the

79. Bread for the World Institute on Hunger and Development, *Hunger 1993,* 115.

80. Hannah Arendt, *The Human Condition* (Chicago: The University of Chicago Press, 1958), 5.

81. L. U. De Sitter, *Op Weg Naar Nieuwe Fabrieken en Kantoren* [Toward New Factories and Offices] (Deventer: Kluwer, 1981).

82. Ibid.

Economic Council of Canada's report *Good Jobs, Bad Jobs* predicts that the 1990s will witness "widening disparities in the quality of jobs and in the degree of economic security they provide for their workers."[83]

It is striking that most discussions about work do not consider whether a restructuring of industry can bring about a recovery of employment. They simply accept ongoing technological development as a given, even though technological development has considerable impact on both the quantity and quality of work. The assumption appears to be that we may not tamper with technological development. But we recognize an element of truth in E. F. Schumacher's observation that "modern technology has deprived people of the kinds of work which they have most enjoyed; creative, useful work requiring one's hands and brainpower. However, the work of mass production is fragmentary; and for the most part people take little pleasure in it."[84]

The realities of both structural unemployment and the dwindling quality of work give us pause. For we live in a society rooted partly in the belief that work is one of the most important of all human activities. In the words of Hannah Arendt, "The modern age has carried with it a theoretical glorification of labor and has resulted in a factual transformation of the whole of society into a laboring society."[85] Is it not then bewildering that this same modern age has also engendered the "prospect of a society of laborers without labor, that is, without the only activity left to them?"[86]

The authors belong to the generation of economists who grew up during the massive unemployment of the depression and the upheaval of the thirties. We were trained in the new economic science, which suggested that we could eliminate unemployment. While not supporting several premises of that economic science, we have sympathy for the principle of full employment. For when everyone who wants to work can work, then economic life has contributed to one's experience of the meaningfulness of human life itself.

It is economists, nonetheless, who are largely responsible for narrowing the concept of work to *paid* work. Work performs many important functions. It helps people to begin and maintain relation-

83. Economic Council of Canada, *Good Jobs, Bad Jobs,* 18.
84. E. F. Schumacher, *Small Is Beautiful* (London: Abacus, 1974), 126.
85. Hannah Arendt, *The Human Condition,* 4.
86. Ibid., 5.

ships, to foster a sense of self-worth and self-esteem, and to assume a place in society and become involved in it. These benefits, however, seem to accrue much more to paid work today than to unpaid work. Often unpaid work offers little prestige. To make matters worse, today even paid work does not always play a positive role in one's life. For many people, work means earning an income, and if they could stop working they would. Much work today appeals not to the whole person but to a piece of a person. This in itself has far-reaching consequences: it is striking, for example, how often the National Conference of Catholic Bishops' *Pastoral Letter on the Economy,* published in 1980, uses the word "suffering" in connection with work.

*　　*　　*

Faced with these realities — rising unemployment even in the midst of economic growth, methods of production that appear inexorably to bring with them the steady elimination of employment, and losses in the quality and prestige of work, especially unpaid work — ought we not to conclude that the present-day *solution* to the progressive debilitation of employment in the industrialized economies remains fundamentally defective? How else are we to explain the apparent imperviousness of unemployment to the remedy of production growth today? How else are we to explain the reality that unemployment appears to have become a *structural* feature of today's industrialized economies? The human tragedy caused by the ongoing debilitation of employment and the apparent inability of current solutions to alleviate unemployment form together the third indication that our economy, both in theory and in practice, requires fundamental renewal.

The need for a new approach to both paid and unpaid labor is therefore becoming urgent. Both the capitalism of today and the socialism of yesterday directly link labor to production. Neither acknowledges, in other words, the reality that labor may have meaning in and of itself. Instead, each locates the meaning of labor in the product of labor. But the people actually involved, as we noted earlier, often experience labor quite differently. Their experience suggests that labor may have an *intrinsic* as well as extrinsic value.

Finally, if labor is becoming more and more scarce, then the relationship between labor and income deserves further consideration.

For example, our system of social security, whose financing depends to a large extent on labor, may require revision. And while we shall discuss the prevailing assumptions about labor, we must also address the degree to which our present economic system will permit the implementation of a renewed approach to labor.

The Changing Nature of International Conflict

Though not part of the central economic issue discussed in this book, the changing nature of international conflict has relevance for our deliberations. For the issue of international conflict is intimately related to the appeal for a new economic agenda voiced by the three economic impasses described above.

Without a doubt the most impressive event of the end of the 1980s was the fall of the Berlin Wall and the Iron Curtain. This marked the end of a period of state terror and of large-scale, systematic human rights violations in Eastern Europe. It exposed the failings of the dominant state-planned economies. But most significantly, it appeared to restore prospects of world peace, since the East/West confrontation had lost its real meaning. The thorn had been removed that had led to an ever-growing arms spiral.

Without wanting to diminish the significance of this event, we must grapple with the baffling fact that within one year the world's nations opted to resume traveling on the path of rising military *insecurity*. Consider, in addition to the Gulf War, the raging conflicts in Bosnia-Hercegovina and among nations of the former East bloc. Shockingly, the enormous arms buildup in the Middle East shortly after the collapse of the Iron Curtain almost outpaced the earlier arms buildup engaged in by the East and West.

While these tensions and buildups are primarily political matters, the Gulf War in particular has significant economic ramifications.

It is important to realize that the global "return of military insecurity" after the Cold War was not an accident. Its roots lay in the conduct not just of some people in the Arab world but also of some in the *Western* world. Economists have shown that access to the mineral resources of the world contains conflict potential the scope of which is entirely unknown. Indeed, with the Gulf War a new element has surfaced: now it is primarily the *affluent* nations, not the poor nations, who find themselves compelled to acquire, with whatever degree of violence is required, guaranteed access to the world's oil fields. Often the wealthy nations — especially the United States — are enormous oil producers themselves. But their own oil production cannot match their much larger oil consumption. Though the United States, for example, ranks second in world oil production, 40 percent of all of the oil it consumes is imported, a reality that accounts for 60 percent of the United States' staggering trade deficit.[87] The wealthy nations thus seek to live beyond the means their own territorial boundaries can provide. But their enormous economic power rests on lame feet. For without guaranteed access to economic resources from other parts of the world, their economies shake at their foundations. The giantism of the world's rich nations enhances the ongoing possibility of international conflict.

The gravity of the Gulf War lies also in the fact that the war preempted the use of scarce resources for the sustaining of life in other parts of the world. This preemption was twofold. First, the countries of the North did not earmark the scarce resources freed up from the former arms buildup for peaceful ends, which the leader of the former Soviet Union, Mr. Gorbachev, had appealed for in a major address at the United Nations (an address that pinpointed reversing the trend of worldwide pollution as one of the most important items requiring action). Second, the non–oil-producing poor countries of the South were forced to help finance the Western arms buildup in the Gulf because of the inevitable effect on oil prices and the Western governments' refusal to raise the taxes of their own citizens for this purpose. In other words, the poor countries had no choice but to help finance the startling global arms buildup, even though they themselves could not provide the basic necessities of life for people within their own borders. The Economic Commission for Africa estimates that in 1990 the increase in African oil import costs caused by the Gulf Crisis totaled $2.7 billion. India estimates that it lost $5.8 billion as a result of the Gulf Crisis; Pakistan, $2.1 billion.[88]

Reciprocal economic interactions such as these occur often. The well-known United Nations report *The Relationship Between Disarma-*

---

87. World Resources Institute, *The 1993 Information Please Environmental Almanac*, 79.
88. Bread for the World Institute on Hunger and Development, *Hunger 1992*, 116, 119.

ment and Development systematically explores various connections between increased arms production and sales and the further entrenchment of world poverty.[89] Indeed, they appear to be so mutually interactive that, as the title of the report indicates, the reverse also holds. In other words, arms reductions, especially by the North, have demonstrable benefits for battling poverty. We see this even from the simple fact that arms escalation in the 1980s increased the capital needs of the governments of the wealthy nations so exorbitantly that it resulted in the substantial rise in interest rates mentioned earlier. This rise, of course, substantially aggravated the burden of debt and loan-payment obligations of the Third World countries.

In his book *Warfare and Welfare,* Nobel prize-winning economist Jan Tinbergen has clearly demonstrated that, though the issue of international conflict directly affects economic processes, contemporary economists ignore it in their own investigations.[90]

Defining a New Economic Agenda

Let us now return to our main theme. The unyielding and deteriorating nature of the human and environmental tragedy described above has brought us to the firm conviction that our economy, both in theory and in practice, must be fundamentally renewed. In the chapters that follow we shall argue that present-day economic theory and practice are incapable of adequately addressing poverty, environmental degeneration, and unemployment. We shall also argue that these impasses reveal critical structural flaws eroding the foundation of our societal order, flaws that become visible in the impact that poverty, environmental degeneration, and unemployment have on humanity. Specifically, the economic impasses of our time have a starkly negative impact on relationships among people and with the creation. They violate justice, community, and peace.

But as we now embark on an investigation of what shape economic renewal ought to take, it is necessary to consider yet another new and baffling economic reality: it may well be that poverty, en-

89. United Nations, Report of the Secretary-General, *The Relationship between Disarmament and Development* (Study Series 5), 1982.
90. Jan Tinbergen and Dietrich Fischer, *Warfare and Welfare: Integrating Security Policy into Socio-Economic Policy* (New York: St. Martin's Press, 1987).

vironmental degeneration, and unemployment may no longer be addressed as isolated entities. To a significant degree, they may now form *one* problem. In the words of *Our Common Future:* "These are not separate crises: an environmental crisis, a development crisis, an energy crisis. They are one."[91] Though these words may sound ominous, they may actually help to give us a certain sense of hope. For if these dilemmas do indeed form one problem, then perhaps we can address them jointly from the perspective of a single solution, a solution that current economic thinking and activity does not and cannot anticipate.

In what follows, we shall submit that today's vexing economic problems, though often described in economic terms, are primarily crises of *culture*. They are partly sociopolitical and partly religious. Strictly speaking, then, they will require more than technical solutions; they will also require *cultural* solutions. In exploring economic renewal and the definition of a new economic agenda, we shall therefore find it important to address the premises or assumptions about life that drive economic theory and practice in Western culture. Indeed, the appeal for economic renewal must include an appeal to embrace different values, values that can serve as a foundation for an analysis whose ultimate aim is to encourage the development of a more humane and sustainable society.

But perhaps an objection arises: Is it legitimate to explore values in today's context? Does not a plea to adopt new values serve to trivialize the gravity of the current situation? For is not the assumption that an embrace of different values will automatically lead to greater humanity and sustainability questionable?

Indeed, we believe that this assumption is questionable. Such an approach, which we may label a kind of "voluntarism," creates a false optimism: an optimism that societal structures simply dance to the tune of our desires and values. Ironically, as we shall see, a form of voluntarism lies at the very heart of our present-day Western society, a voluntarism driven by the one-sided value that if everyone simply pursues economic self-interest, then we shall automatically achieve "the greatest happiness for the greatest number."

The plea for adopting different values must therefore also

91. World Commission on Environment and Development, *Our Common Future,* 4.

address the issue of how economic power and control are exercised in our society. The structure of economic control today must play a significant role in our discussions and recommendations. Of course, certain new values — such as the recognition of the value of the other person and of mutual responsibility — imply new power relationships. Likewise, when we work side by side with people whose needs are unmet because of the manner in which our society operates, then new perspectives on forming new power relationships may open up. Consequently, when we urge society to alleviate poverty and dependence, to implement a responsible environmental practice, and to open up our employment system so that it offers a place to everyone in society, we must do so from the vantage point of the disenfranchised and from the desire to voice the interests of those who now have no voice.

The plea to adopt different values must bind itself to those who suffer under the present structures and the values that undergird them. But we must then also seek to renew the current exercise of economic control in our society, and in the following chapters we shall offer several concrete proposals suggesting more precisely *how* we might do so.

CHAPTER 2

Risky Calculations

In Chapter 1 we discussed poverty, environmental degeneration, and structural unemployment together. We shall now explore the possibility, alluded to at the end of Chapter 1, that they *belong* together. Is it possible that these three most significant economic impasses of our time have a common origin and that their simultaneous emergence is not accident?

Chapter 1 highlighted how paradoxical and unyielding these three pressing problems have become. They have become immense and overwhelming; they have acquired such an inner rigidity that many people have the feeling that something fundamental has gone wrong somewhere. It may feel as if we are passengers on a train that somewhere along the way went down the wrong track.

Or, perhaps more aptly, it may feel as if someone must have made a calculation that came out wrong. It is as if a calculation was drafted on behalf of our society, and our society has been working out the calculation in economic practice for years under the assumption that it would produce a favorable outcome. However, precisely now that the moment of truth has arrived, the calculation no longer appears to add up. To make matters worse, we seem to lack an opportunity to redo the calculation. For developments in the areas of poverty, environmental degeneration, and unemployment seem to happen at such breakneck speed and on such a global scale that they appear to be out of control. The burden of debt still hangs like a dark cloud over the poorest countries of our world, and our monetary system is so fundamentally unstable that even a minor shock causes it to shudder at its foundations. And social and military instability continues to increase.

Using this image of a calculation, let us propose a thesis. Perhaps the trio of economic impasses described in Chapter 1 have their origin in a massive social calculation drafted by the *science of economics* and presented to society for implementation. Unfortunately, however, when put into *economic practice,* the calculation appears to lead to a perpetuation of poverty, the ruin of nature, and a rise in structural unemployment.

We shall test the validity of that thesis in this chapter. Our aim here is not to bring accusations against economic thinking as such. Rather, it is to focus on the *linkages* between economic theory and practice. We shall explore the myriad connections that link economic theory and practice, connections we are often scarcely aware of. Is it not at least conceivable that enormous problems might arise in economic practice because unsound theories and assumptions about life support the economic actions of people who are simply acting in good faith? Further, societal orders historically appear often to evoke and then entrench precisely that type of economic thought that assures their own survival. If this is the case today, then will not the economic thought that has emerged today obscure the reality of certain problems, and will it not serve several fixed economic interests rather than the interests of the entire population?

We therefore consider it critical to explore the premises or assumptions that drive economic thought today. This ought to lead us back to the sources of the concrete problems described in Chapter 1. Moreover, it will create room for the entrance of other perspectives and approaches; and these will be sorely needed if we are to find different solutions than the ready prescriptions dispensed by currently accepted economic thought. In brief, we may describe the economic perspective defended in this book as *the caring administration of what has been entrusted to us* (the original meaning of the word *economics*), an *economics of care,* or an *economics of enough.* With "caring administration" as our starting point, an entirely different economic scenario emerges than the one provided by an economy whose trademark is the pursuit of more and more material prosperity measured in money. By now this trademark identifies not only our economy but also our society itself.

In this chapter we shall first explore the "calculation" that classical economists drafted and recommended to the society of their time. Then we shall consider the doctrine of contemporary neoclassical economists and explore how that doctrine has perhaps obscured the reality of today's pressing local and global problems. Finally, throughout we hope to have nudged our thinking sufficiently toward a renewal of economic thought to inspect the three major problems flagged in Chapter 1 with somewhat better vision.

The Calculation of Classical Economic Thought

Classical economic thought is one or two centuries old. The reason for turning to it briefly is that classical economic thought laid the groundwork for the calculation that most of Western society now endorses. A strain within classical thinking, Utilitarianism, even adopted as its primary objective the making of a calculation for society as a whole. Utilitarianism recommended a "felicific calculus."

The felicific calculus was in essence very simple. Utilitarianism saw human happiness as a question of adding up what was pleasurable and subtracting what was painful, or of adding utilities and subtracting disutilities. Working within this philosophical and ethical tradition, the later classical economists identified the flow of all marketable goods as a stream of "utilities," and the labor used to produce these goods, with all of its drudgery, as a basic "disutility."

This "happiness equation" had immense impact! For immediately it led to the conclusion that human happiness is best served when a given input of labor produces as much output as possible. And millions in our society *today* regard this conclusion, a conclusion that equates a rise in the productivity of labor with an increase in happiness, as a self-evident truth. Indeed, it more or less forms the heart of the economic order in which we now live. But a number of premises or assumptions, each of which is disputable and perhaps dangerous, lurk within it. One such premise is that happiness is not something we *receive* but only something we can *achieve*. A second premise is that the source of happiness lies directly in the amount of goods and services produced and sold in the market. And a third premise is that because less human work means more leisure time, the less work we do the better off we are.

Utilitarianism is thus the first example of an economic thinking that is intimately related to the fabric of our society and to the directives by which it operates. More poignantly, however, it also obscures the reality of certain problems as they crop up. For according to this economic approach, *less* work, *less* employment, as long as it does not lead to a drop in production, is a *benefit*.

A second calculation made by classical economic thought has had a comparable influence on us today. It suggests that we must follow the *market* wherever it leads, because the market will act as our guide to a better future for all. Naturally, for this to succeed, we must permit the market to do its work with as little disruption and political interference as possible.

Adam Smith, the theoretical founder of this vision, spoke more humanely than many of his later followers. Faced with the abject poverty of his time, Smith inquired how the wealth of the nations, including that of the poor living in his own society, could be increased. Impressed by the scientific achievements of his day, especially by new production techniques, he identified two fundamental forces of production that he believed would lead all of society to increased prosperity: the division of labor and the accumulation of capital. For Smith, the real wellspring of prosperity lay in the division or specialization of labor, which was made possible by the progress of industrial technology and by infusions of capital. But this wellspring could flow and have its beneficial effects only in and through the market. Because mass production requires large numbers of buyers, buyers who by definition are therefore anonymous, the optimal division of labor could occur only through the unrestrained operation of market forces. Only through the "expansion of the market" could entrepreneurs bring in enough capital to organize production processes and to supply enough machinery to create the necessary division of labor.

For Smith, the market was therefore the key to a better and more prosperous future. It was the institution by which human progress in technology and economics became visible. Not only that, but the market offered a way of measuring human progress (using prices and quantities) and of spreading progress around the globe. Indeed, for Smith the market played a role in *all* forms of human progress. It stimulated industriousness, culture, and the desire to save. Moreover, the market itself, led as if by an invisible hand, ensured the participation of the poor in the expanding wealth. Smith believed that the spontaneous operation of the market led economic processes "by an

44

invisible hand to make nearly the same distribution of the necessaries of life, which would have been made, had the earth been divided into equal portions among all its inhabitants."[1]

Is this an outmoded or dead vision? Most definitely not! It has been transfused into the bloodstream of our Western culture. Consciously or unconsciously we live it out in our society and propagate it around the world. We recognize in it the backdrop to many well-known premises undergirding our economic practice today. One such premise is that, as much as possible, the market must operate free of government interference. Indeed, the free working of the market lies close to the heart of Western society's self-definition: in the West it is not a government's place to tamper with the market, because this signifies a step away from a free society and toward a totalitarian society. A second premise operating today is that if a Third World country genuinely desires material prosperity, it must demonstrate its resolve by declaring that it is "open for business" and that the free market economy is welcome within its borders; it must then permit the money economy to rapidly replace the informal economy. And a third premise is that when we allow the market to do its sovereign work, then every poor person has the opportunity to get out of poverty.

All of these are deeply held premises or assumptions; in other words, they adhere to the choices that people make, to visions of life, and even to the contents of one's faith. And in our time, after the breakdown of the planned economies in the former communist countries, they possess enough vitality to present themselves as untouchable truths.

In our assessment, however, these premises are not just questionable, they are misleading. They are misleading in content, displaying the colors of the Enlightenment's naive belief in human progress and of a Deist vision of society. They have as their undertone the mechanist worldview that suggests that a good society must function like a machine whose operation is controlled by the laws of nature. And they show the texture of the more recent modern capitalism, whereby positive capital return automatically indicates the social desirability of a particular project.

More strikingly, however, these premises are also misleading in

---

1. Quoted by Andrew Skinner in his Introduction to Adam Smith, *The Wealth of Nations* (Harmondsworth, England: Penguin Books Ltd., 1970), 27.

their demonstrable effects, for their effects coincide with the economic predicaments described in Chapter 1. The classical economic approach sanctions the "enlightened" self-interest of the individual as the cornerstone of all economic activity, and by definition it disqualifies any government intervention in the market. If, then, by listening to the voice of self-interest and obeying the dictates of the free market we benefit the poor just as if the earth had been "divided into equal portions among all its inhabitants," why concern ourselves with the *division* of the expanding prosperity? Why also concern ourselves with the state of the environment or with unemployment if, as the classical approach assumes, the operation of the natural order permits humanity unrestricted cultivation of the earth and if the operation of the market spontaneously increases employment? Indeed, armed with these assumptions about the world and about life, why trouble ourselves over a lopsided division of wealth, over the destruction of the environment, or over the structural unemployment that eventually arises? The classical economic approach renders these concerns redundant and eases a guilty conscience in advance.

Modern economic science was launched with this calculation of market and self-interest. It went hand in glove with the new social order, or with the "new social fabric" (the term of Carl Becker) that began at the same time. It was no accident that not until around 1850 did governments put into place the first serious corrections of production methods and of numerous other effects of the new economic order — such as the living conditions of the poor, the work hours of women and children, and the lack of any form of social assistance. For the science of economics had been silent about these forms of economic mismanagement. Even today, it approaches economic reality not primarily in terms of *care,* but in terms of the individual's pursuit of material prosperity.

Labor as a Calculation

Protest, critique, and the search for an alternative to this calculation came from another quarter: that of Karl Marx and Friedrich Engels. For them, pauperization, poverty, and exploitation were genuine economic realities. Marx in particular attempted to uncover capitalism's laws of development. He formulated these laws in an economic

46

theory that loads nearly every term with "evil": a laborer is a "wage-slave," wages are equal to "the reproduction value of the labor force," and an enterprise's amount of profit is directly related to the "degree of exploitation" involved. Marx and Engels argued that this was how capitalism deformed economic reality. Capitalism, they believed, turned people into objects, made work a form of enslavement, and alienated people not only from their social and natural surroundings but also from themselves. Can one, then, conceive of a greater contrast with the premises of classical economics?

Yet we must be cautious here. It was for good reason that John Hicks called Karl Marx "the last of the classics." Though Marx whole-heartedly rejected the theory that the sovereign operation of the market benefits all, and though he considered private property the root of all alienation, he was convinced that capitalism fulfills a "his-torical mission" as a social form. He further believed that nothing is impossible for modern technology, that it is the use of tools that distinguishes humanity from the animal world (humanity is "a tool-making animal"), and that the transition to a communist society is possible only on the basis of a full fledged automated production system. The poor will get their opportunity — but only in the context of belonging to the working class, which by definition is exploited; the environment will receive attention, certainly — but only in the context of human manipulation of it. For according to Marx, no economic value can effectively come into being unless human labor is its source.

Therefore, it is incorrect to expect that Marxist economics and the economic order whose arrival it proclaims will cause the three major problems discussed in Chapter 1 to vanish from the face of the earth. Neither in theory nor in practice has it emphasized, nor can it emphasize, the need to establish standards for technological develop-ment or to suspend economic expansion before all forces of produc-tion have been developed. Even less evident is a vision of humanity and the environment that would prevent them from being turned into objects of progress. We may say that in a certain sense, while Smith expected human well-being to spring from the sovereign activity of the market, Marx expected human well-being to spring from the sovereign development of the forces of production, the fruits of which would come to the labor class by means of the class struggle. But for *both* Smith and Marx it is *labor* that produces human well-being, and for both, human well-being consists primarily in the abundance of produced material goods, thanks to an unfettered application of industrial technology.[2]

Neoclassical Thought:
Thought Lacking a Calculation?

Classical economic thinkers recommended "calculations" about how a human society can become prosperous. Certain connections link these calculations to our daily thinking and action, to Western people in our day, connections we are hardly aware of. But do similar connections link modern, *neoclassical* economic thinking with our daily thinking and activity? And do they hinder or hamper us from finding genuine ways out of the crises of our time?

It is not as easy to answer this question as it is to describe the influence exercised by classical thought today. For since its inception, modern, neoclassical economic thought has attempted to protect itself from the reproach that it is making the "value-laden" attempt to recommend a specific direction for society to take. In modern economic thought we no longer find well-formulated calculations and recommendations about how we can become wealthy together. The responsibility for this question has devolved to a separate branch of science: "welfare economics" now must handle this thorny question. Modern economics attempts merely to offer *explanations,* just as the natural sciences attempt merely to explain reality, as it searches for universally valid laws and undeniable facts that can be linked together in an objective and unbiased fashion. So it may seem that we cannot accuse modern economists of holding dangerous or unacceptable premises and biases, or of attempting to ease and allay the consciences of affluent people and societies. For these have no place in a "value-free" science.

Or is neoclassical economic thought less innocent and value-free than it appears?

2. For a more detailed discussion of the issues raised in this section, see Bob Goudzwaard, *Capitalism and Progress: A Diagnosis of Western Society,* trans. and ed. Josina van Nuis Zylstra (Toronto: Wedge Publishing Foundation; Grand Rapids: William B. Eerdmans Publishing Company, 1979).

Enter a Philosopher

The answer to this question arrives when we explore how the search for a value-free economic science came about, and at what price. And the origin of this pursuit lies not with Adam Smith but with one of the most significant philosophers of the Enlightenment: Immanuel Kant.

One cannot do justice to Kant in a brief discussion. Yet we must consider something of his thought, because it affects all of us greatly.

Immanuel Kant was a philosopher who wrestled for his entire life with the question of how reliable, objective knowledge is "universally possible." He sought knowledge that is not sullied or influenced by personal emotions or value judgments. Kant began by arguing that what we perceive of the world around us is ultimately nothing more than a "chaos of sense impressions." Then he wondered: can we obtain any genuine knowledge out of this chaos?

At first glance Kant's answer appears modest. He stated that we can never actually know reality — the "thing in itself." But, he added, we can order our sense impressions, or give them an order. For example, we can distinguish between what comes first and what comes next in time, and between what differs spatially. We can also ascertain whether one phenomenon causes another. In this manner Kant developed his doctrine of categories. Categories, for Kant, are principles by which one orders the chaos of sense impressions. Through the categories knowledge arises that is not clouded by personal, subjective elements. In other words, through the categories genuine science is born.

What is striking is that a certain form of calculation or bias is not alien to Kant himself. He makes an attempt to return to the simplest elements (in this case, sense impressions) in order to rebuild the world from them in thought, as it were. Kant does not begin with a creation that has an order and that has been entrusted to us by its Creator. Rather, he begins with a chaos above which broods the Spirit of Reason, as the beginning of all order. But what that Spirit orders is not yet a human society. It orders so that it can gather *objective knowledge,* knowledge that drives science.

Yet it would seem that this calculation is entirely different than one intended for society as a whole. Or is there a bridge between them?

Let us examine how the followers of Kant applied his ideas to economics during and after 1870. Like Kant, economists like Carl Menger and Max Weber pursued "genuine knowledge": in this case, genuine objective economic knowledge. But arriving at genuine objective economic knowledge is notably more difficult with economic phenomena than with physical phenomena. Under given circumstances a stone always falls at the same speed. But when it comes to the economic behavior of people, if the price of butter rises, one consumer buys more while another buys less. Human behavior is capricious and ignores static, natural laws. How then is it possible to arrive at science, at knowledge that is predictable and certain?

Faced with this question, the followers of Kant in economics took a similar tack to their master's. If certainty does not lie within the given facts themselves, then one must *construct* a thought space that makes certainty possible! The followers of Kant needed to accomplish one feat to construct this thought space: they needed to work out of or expel from the field of study of economics all economic changes and developments that contain a seed of uncertainty. They needed to arrive at the point where all that remains for analysis and explanation in their science is what is certain and what one can make positive statements about.

Here we stand at the cradle of what modern economics calls the "data circle." Data are given factors or states of affairs that economics as such does *not* study, because it cannot make statements about their development with certainty. Human needs, motives, and desires belong to such data, which the neo-Kantian Strigl once called "economic categories," in the footsteps of Kant's overall project.[3] The economist establishes that someone wants butter, as well as the amount wanted, but he or she does not seek to *understand* this desire; it forms merely a given. Other such data (that is, given factors or starting points for economic explanation) include the nature and composition of the population, the state of technology at a particular moment, the existing social order, and nature. The question of how or why these factors develop is referred to a practitioner of a different science as quickly as possible. The task is to study only what functions within the given circle or domain of factors, which means that the

3. R. Strigl, *Die Ökonomische Kategorieën und die Organisation der Wirtschaft* (Jena: Gustav Fischer, 1923).

economist is restricted to analyzing only those entities that can be measured. In other words, the economist must confine himself or herself to analyzing strictly the processes of the *market mechanism*. The issues therefore include the question of what prices change, whether the economy produces less or more, how much investment and economic growth will increase, and what wages will do. The economist can make so-called objective statements and formulate laws about these. As soon as the economist knows what people's needs are, or what the maximum return (or whatever else) that the entrepreneur seeks is, what technological expertise is available, and so forth, he or she can begin to work. Based on these *given* factors, the economist can explain objectively and scientifically the operation of the market mechanism with 100 percent accuracy, just as a true natural scientist would. But the economist should never try to understand the data that surrounds him or her in the data circle, because such an attempt would damage or destroy the objectivity and certainty of the conclusions.

A Distorted Worldview

That was not an easy interlude. But it was necessary in order to answer the question of how modern, neoclassical economic thinking may have gone off track. Neoclassical economic thought has done almost everything it can to present itself as a positive (Hutchison, Friedman), neutral (Robbins), or objective science. To do so, economists have had to expel from their own field of investigation all forms of uncertainty about economic facts and relationships. They have had to "work these away" to the data circle. But what a heavy price the science of economics has paid for this! Because of its drive to become value free, modern economics has lost value and credibility on at least four fronts.

Economic Needs

The first front is human *economic needs*. Economic science considers them capricious by nature, and it argues that any assessment of needs based on their own merits contains value judgments. Because it wants nothing to do with value judgments, economics merely accepts all needs as "given," as data; it accepts them as they present themselves

51

to the market, with no further questions asked. The same holds true for the desires and pursuits of entrepreneurs, unions, and governments. To economics as a positive science, economic needs and material desires form merely a point of departure, not a point of discussion.

Oddly enough, however, modern economics reserves for itself exclusive authority to render judgments about the efficiency of the *means* employed to meet these needs! Why is efficiency desirable? Does not a value judgment lie here? More importantly, do not human needs and choices themselves contain an economic aspect that economics as a science ought to investigate? If people can select *means* uneconomically, then can they not select *ends* or needs uneconomically? For example, is it not possible that satisfying the needs of one group or one society might jeopardize the ability to meet the needs of another group or society? In other words, if economics as a science can easily and uncritically accept as the starting point for analysis every need presented to the market, then does it not *legitimize* needs in a certain sense? And because only those with buying power can register needs in the market, does it not legitimize the limitless needs of the *rich* in particular?

Our skepticism rises when we read in virtually every economic textbook that human needs are unlimited or infinite by nature. Consider whether this is true. If it were, then the whole earth, with all that it contains, would fall short of meeting the needs of just a few people. But surely this is a thoroughly Western, Faustian idea! We encounter here the thought pattern undergirding what Tawney has called the "acquisitive society," a society that not only never has "enough" but also gives its own needs priority over other needs.[4]

Therefore the first loss suffered because of economics' attempt to become a value-free science is that economics no longer permits any form of "needs criticism." Even when such criticism is economically motivated, economists immediately refer it to ethics or political science.

Nature and the Environment

The acceptance of the neoclassical approach further means that *nature* and the *environment* become data. Consequently, they fall outside the

4. See Richard H. Tawney, *The Acquisitive Society* (Brighton: Wheatsheaf, 1982).

direct study and concern of economics. Economic analysis takes into account the state of the environment only *after* economic agents add environmental protection to their list of economic needs and register this by spending scarce means on it. The neoclassical defense of this practice is that changes in the natural environment belong to the field of biology, not economics. But does this apply even when the processes of production and consumption cause changes to occur in flora, fauna, the atmosphere, and the condition of the soil? Does it also apply when changes in flora, fauna, the atmosphere, and the condition of the soil have consequences for the processes of production and consumption? The answer given by neoclassical theory is that any "external effects" affecting production and consumption, such as changes in the environment, belong to the study of economics only if they cause a direct, objectively verifiable economic depreciation of scarce means, that is, of existing consumption or capital goods.

But here, too, we must speak of a real loss of the value and credibility of modern-day economics. For innumerable forms of production and consumption today cause tremendous long-term environmental destruction — destruction that escapes the attention of ourselves and our governments. To the extent that we do not register the remediation of this destruction on our list of economic needs, neoclassical economics does not consider it a direct, objectively verifiable economic loss. As a result, it does not enter the field of investigation of economics.

Yet are not human living space and human health just as legitimate economic "objects" as a car or a dishwasher? In the modern economic framework they are not. For if modern economics were to concede that these are indeed legitimate economic objects, then it would also have to concede that we can economically squander nature, health, and the environment. And then economic science could no longer consider all such environmental components as given, uninterrogated data simply presented to the science of economics for analysis.

We see, then, that the modern science of economics recognizes only one kind of economic object for study: objects of use. Entities related to production or consumption receive an economic value (price) only when they are paid for and used. But the economic tasks of people and societies include more than simply producing and consuming; they also include *care*. Care is an authentic element of the

53

oldest definitions of the Greek word *oikonomia*, or *economy*. *Oikonomia* means the *care* of the economist or steward for the household *(oikos)* and for that which is entrusted to him or her within the household. With this definition of economics, it is no longer self-evident that human health, the environment, and the natural resources poised for extraction fall outside of the domain of economic objects. For now economic objects include objects of care. Economic life consists of more than producing and consuming; it consists also of sustaining and keeping.

Economic Accountability

Modern economics' relentless effort to define itself as a neutral science has a third consequence: the neoclassical economic approach eliminates the possibility of *economic accountability*.

Let us explore this issue for a moment. If economics explains all human needs, desires, and objectives as givens whose rationality or origin economics itself does not investigate, then what happens to the study of economic life and activity? Only the results of human action expressed in prices and quantities remain for investigation. Only a kind of mechanism remains: a system of gears and sprockets of "economic variables" in which people themselves, as living beings, disappear. Certainly, economic science includes individuals, organizations, and entrepreneurs in its explanations. It even identifies them by name. But they are not "living" realities; rather, economic science "mummifies" them, as it were. They more or less become automatons who in a given, presupposed manner simply react to the facts as they present themselves. Economic processes run through them, as it were, as water runs through a downspout.

We may describe this phenomenon in another way. When modern economics must explain something — such as an increase in unemployment, a slowdown of economic growth, or a rise in inflation — it never raises the question of *who* has caused the change or to whom it must be ascribed. Only the question of *what* the unemployment, slow growth, or inflation has set in motion is in order. Modern economics never views people, organizations, businesses, or unions as the actual cause of economic destruction. In the words of John Hicks: "Causality is a matter of explanation; but when we explain, we do not necessarily praise or condemn."[5] Praising and condemning have no place in a positive, neutral science.

But again we must state: how damaging it is, and what a loss for economics and society as a whole, that modern economic thought rejects any possibility of assigning the responsibility for economic damages and ailments to their economic agents! The theory of economic policy refuses to consider the economic benefit or harm that *people* do to others as such; rather, it understands economic benefit and harm solely as effects of the good or bad functioning of the market mechanism itself. As a result, in practice economic policy usually attacks only the symptoms, not the real cause of economic misdoing. It remains entirely silent, for example, when a business jacks up prices or when a union demands too much. Without a means for economic accountability, modern economics accepts everyone and everyone's desires uncritically and without question — within, of course, existing laws. But in so doing modern economic theory fully accommodates itself to our social order, an order whose deepest structural principle has become this: "Always obtain more for oneself."

Human Labor

The fourth damaging effect of modern economics' drive to become a positive and value-free science is that our society's view of *labor* has changed. For classical economists, labor still functioned as the origin or source of all economic value. no value could come into existence other than that which came through human work. But modern economics pushes human labor from the center to the periphery. Labor is now nothing more than one of several production factors. And like land and capital, the two other important production factors, labor receives its economic value from the market. Without a market value, work has no value.

This way of viewing work — work as a paid production factor — is not only thoroughly familiar to us, it is in our blood, as it were. It therefore presents itself in ironclad logic, though we must add that it is the reigning economic system that constructs and defines that logic. But understood from within an economic perspective broader

5. John Hicks, *Causality in Economics* (Oxford: Blackwell, 1979), 7.

than that of scarcity measured in prices, such as the perspective of *caring administration,* this approach to labor creates a serious reduction in at least two respects.

The first reduction lies in the valuation of labor. In the modern framework labor is "instrumental." Work has economic value only to the extent to which it generates an income and functions as an instrument for producing goods and services, and only to the extent to which others have money to buy the goods and services produced. But does this tell the complete economic story about work? Where is the acknowledgment of what Max Weber called "the intrinsic value of labor"? Where is the recognition that labor has value because it is *human* labor, irrespective of its financial accomplishments? Human well-being depends a great deal on the quality of work; indeed, the quality of work can make or break a person both bodily and spiritually, as it were. Therefore, economically speaking, we must see labor as more than a means of production. Because it is *human* labor it is an economic object in another sense: it is an object of *care.* What applies to the environment applies equally to human work, namely, that if we do not take care of it, if we treat it only instrumentally, then inevitably we have created a fundamental economic loss.

According to neoclassical economics, however, unless financial compensation has been arranged, one cannot include the loss of the quality of work among economic losses. Without compensation it is ungraspable; it is not sufficiently measurable and thus does not belong to the domain of economics. For the modern economist, the quality of work has significance only if people attempt to use their scarce resources to improve it. As long as people do not spend money on it, our economist has no interest in hearing about an economic necessity for preserving the intrinsic value of work. According to him or her, every such broader concern belongs to ethics, not economics.

A second reduction about labor occurs when one pushes labor from the center to the periphery. It has to do with the kinds of work that people choose to do. According to modern economics, in order to call something *labor* in the full sense of the word, it must be registered in a market: the labor market. Real work is therefore paid work. Without a price tag, neoclassical economics cannot distinguish labor from activities done in one's leisure time. Real economic labor is therefore paid — paid at the price that management and labor have collectively agreed upon.

But we must assert instead that perhaps the most important

56

forms of labor are unpaid. Here, too, one's economic approach —
whether one adopts the approach of scarcity measured in prices or of
caring administration — is decisive. Many forms of human work
orient themselves to the care and keeping of culture and the environment. They do not orient themselves primarily to producing something for the market but to the nurture and development of people,
social relationships, and ecosystems through time. Understood within
the perspective of care, work that produces products for the market
we may call *directly productive labor;* work that orients itself to the care
and keeping of life through time we may call *transductive labor.*

Transductive labor can be paid or unpaid. It includes such
diverse activities as raising children, sustaining the environment,
caring for and maintaining other people, performing in music and
theater, acquiring an education, and improving both urban and rural
landscapes. The work of government departments and ministries also
belongs to the transductive sector. Part of what links all of these forms
of transductive labor together, whether paid or unpaid, is that they do
not orient themselves primarily toward increasing production and that
they do not automatically bring with them their own financial return.
They do not spontaneously earn their keep by way of the market.
They can receive a financial reward, if people have so agreed ahead
of time — a reward that we call something other than a wage (a salary,
an honorarium, a reimbursement for costs, for example) and that
people from elsewhere, such as from the directly productive sector,
must pay for, either voluntarily or through other means.

Current economic thinking has the tendency to neglect the intrinsic economic value and significance of transductive labor. The
reason is that transductive labor orients itself to the care and maintenance of the data in the data circle, and the modern economist does
not include such care and maintenance among his or her concerns.
Instead, for him or her every emphasis lies on generating production
streams to reduce the relative scarcity of goods and services registered
by the market. The modern economist recognizes transductive labor
only if it is paid or reimbursed. But the shortsightedness of this
approach surfaces when we realize that the streams of goods and
services generated by directly productive labor damage, with great
ease, the stocks and stores of resources, ecosystems, human health,
and cultural heritage that still exist in today's world. When such
damage to the data occurs, transductive labor becomes *more* important

instead of *less* important. Ought we not to learn a lesson from the so-called informal sector of the poor countries, namely, that it is unpaid transductive labor that keeps society afloat, and that the uniqueness and identity of a culture often lie here?

The distinction between productive and transductive labor sheds light on two of the economic paradoxes we encountered in Chapter 1: the paradoxes of decreasing care and decreasing labor in the midst of increasing material wealth. Directly productive labor orients itself to the market sector, and in the market sector people make strenuous efforts to continuously increase productivity (remember the utilitarian calculation of classical economic thought). Rising productivity means that more products are produced by the same number of workers or in the same number of work hours. In principle, the rising productivity of the production process makes possible higher incomes per capita each year, especially in the so-called advanced sectors of the economy. As productivity rises, the wage and salary levels of directly productive labor also rise. But modern society scarcely tolerates significant differentials in the increases of wages. As a result, each year we typically use potential wage increases in the *advanced* sectors of the economy as a standard for *general* across-the-board increases in wages and salaries in our society.

However, in the care sectors of the economy, such as health, education, and welfare, sectors that rely heavily on transductive labor, it is impossible to enforce the productivity increases possible in the advanced sectors of the economy. In fact, demanding continuous increases in worker productivity in hospitals, schools, and social work settings can destroy this relationship-centered work. As a result, every year the gap widens between what the care sectors *must* pay employees (because of the wage and salary standards of society) and what they are *able* to pay them (because of the slow rise in productivity in these sectors). This widening gap means that, though the prices of industrial products are able to remain the same or drop, due to increased production efficiency, the costs and prices of services in the care sectors of society increase each year. Indeed, as we see increasingly today, the costs of care become so expensive that they even become partially unpayable, certainly in terms of the public funds that society as a whole can designate for transductive services. This in turn has the effect of driving labor out of the paid transductive sector, in proportion to the rising gap in productivity between the care and advanced sectors of the economy.

This creates the labor paradox: in rapidly expanding economies,

58

a continuous rise in productivity simultaneously *increases* care needs but *decreases* the available volume of paid transductive labor required to meet those needs.

We shall return to this paradox in Chapter 5. But already here we may identify a grim by-product of our society's increasing inability to meet care needs. As we saw with the poverty paradox in Chapter 1, certain forms of poverty have reappeared and will reappear in the midst of wealthy societies. As is well known, what is relevant for the emergence of poverty is not just the amount of social assistance moneys available but also the cost of living and the level of unemployment. Both of these tend to rise as the costs of care rise. In this context, the "fixed" living costs of every household are critical. Higher costs for medical care and education directly affect the level of poverty of poor families. And the more the costs of care increase in relation to the drop in price of industrial products, the more people on the poor side of society will become squeezed.

Revisiting Poverty, the Environment, and Unemployment

We have now assembled enough elements and ingredients — such as the economic necessity of care and transductive labor, the distinction between needs that are registered and needs that are not registered by the market, the intrinsic value of labor and of the environment, and the need for economic accountability — for us to consider whether together they provide a better optic by which to view the origin of, and possibly the solution to, the trio of problems identified in Chapter 1.

Throughout, it has become clear that neoclassical economic thinking cannot actually help us with these economic dilemmas of our time. Because it operates in terms of the market, it misses entirely the large shards of poverty that the market is unable to register; because it approaches scarcity solely in terms of prices, it is unable to assess the economic value of the ecological problem; and because it views labor solely as a paid production factor, it bypasses today's quantity and quality of work problem. Neoclassical economics was not designed to help solve these problems. It seeks to understand and support only that which relates to the streams of production, consumption, income, and money in a market economy.

Therefore, by means of alternative economic concepts, we shall attempt, however falteringly, to understand how these three pressing problems might have structurally embedded themselves in our world society. To begin, we offer the following diagram, which also utilizes elements from the thinking of economists such as Fred Hirsch, Herman Daly, and others:[6]

Beginning "Stocks"

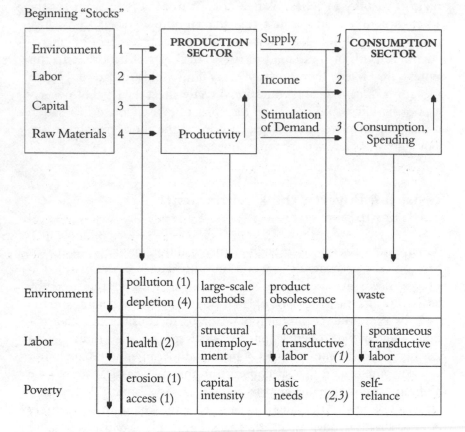

6. See Fred Hirsch, *Dilemmas of Liberal Democracies: Studies in Fred Hirsch's Social Limits to Growth,* ed. Adrian Ellis and Krishan Kumar (London: Tavistock Publications, 1983); Herman E. Daly, *Steady State Economics* (Washington, D.C.: Island Press, 1991); Herman E. Daly and John B. Cobb, *For the Common Good: Redirecting the Economy Toward Community, the Environment, and a Sustainable Future* (Boston: Beacon Press, 1989).

In the top section one can see that in our economic order production factors are combined with production processes. The results then find their way into the consumption sector in the form of goods and services. The production process uses environmental factors that are partly unpaid; and production must create income to make consumption possible. On the production side, continually escalating production assumes a steady increase in the productivity of the production process. And on the consumption side, continually escalating production makes necessary an influencing of demand through advertising in order to ensure a sufficient market for products.

On the bottom is a threefold bar whose headings describe, in terms of the perspective of caring administration, the effects on people, culture, and the environment of the processes outlined on the top. It highlights the "preservation," or "stock," side of society, as it were, focusing on where increased production, consumption, and income acquisition cause shifts to occur in the nature and scope of care needs. The diagram divides these effects into the trio of problems identified in Chapter 1, with bars showing the effects on the environment, labor, and poverty.

The first bar, that of the environment, shows that progressively increasing production has the effect of damaging the quality of the natural environment. Rapidly increasing production and consumption extracts and depletes raw materials and energy from the environment and returns waste and pollution to it. Increased production and large-scale production methods (for example, aggressive, large-scale, and monocultural methods of working the land) intensify these harmful environmental effects as much as stimulating demand does (by, for example, shortening the life expectancy of products and making disposable products). The combination of all of these effects led Herman Daly to call our societal production "throughput." Beginning stocks are "rushed" through the streams of production and consumption at an ever-higher tempo.

The second bar, that of labor, presents a similarly troublesome picture. A continual increase in productivity directly damages the stocks of spiritual and bodily health by overemphasizing the "use" dimension of human work and underemphasizing the quality of work. But as we alluded to in Chapter 1, a continual increase in productivity also means that, in order to prevent a loss of jobs, the overall rise in *production* must remain at least as great, percentage-wise, as the increase of *productivity*. In other words, as soon as the growth of the gross national product (GNP) falls below the average increase of productivity per laborer for the same year, a loss of jobs occurs. For example, if in a given year the GNP rises by 3 percent but the average increase of productivity rises by 5 percent, then a loss of jobs in the amount of 2 percent occurs. In addition, as we saw earlier with the labor paradox, the income escalation made possible by production growth has the effect of decreasing the volume of transductive labor, because in its paid form it becomes too expensive. Finally, increased income and consumption have an effect, identified by Hirsh and others, on the available *time* of consumers. People have less and less time, and as a result the time that people have for spontaneous and voluntary transductive labor decreases.

In short, an ever-increasing rise in the production of material goods in an already wealthy society indeed has the paradoxical consequence that there is continually *more* work to do at the level of caring for the environment and for other people, but the opportunities for exercising this care continually decrease! This holds true for both paid and unpaid transductive labor. When combined with the negative effect that increased production efficiency may have on employment levels in the directly productive sector, the total effect on the supply of jobs may very well be negative.

The third bar shows something of the consequences of our continual production fury for the poor nations of the Third World. If one looks only at the top section of the diagram, one notes a positive and optimistic result for the Third World: greater demand by the wealthy nations jacks up economic growth in the Third World, while the production supplied by "our" transnational corporations there creates employment. But the bottom part of the diagram shows several countervailing effects on the poor nations: the rapid depletion of raw materials, which the poor countries can no longer use to meet their own needs; the use of large-scale, inappropriate, and capital-intensive technologies, which causes employment growth to stagnate; the occupation of land, which drives small farmers off of their land, destroys communities, and in general decreases access to the poor nations' own resources; and an income distribution and stimulation of demand through advertising that satisfy the luxury needs of some but that, in so doing, reduce opportunities for others to meet their own subsistence needs. Finally, rapidly emerging modernization in the Third

62

World has the effect of attacking and debilitating the informal sector and its transductive labor.

Here, too, we draw the conclusion that an economic approach that takes as its starting point the *care* needed to sustain people and the environment offers a much clearer explanation than the current theories do for why the poor become poorer even in the midst of rapid modernization.

Finally, the reader may add a fourth bar showing the consequences of a continual growth in production and consumption for peace and security throughout the world. Here the rising export of arms and the stronger demand for strategic resources and minerals have a negative impact on international security.

Locating a Solution

Let us assume for a moment that this approach as a whole is correct and that we can explain the deterioration and rigidification of poverty, environmental degeneration, and unemployment in today's world in this manner. Does this approach then also help us to locate a solution to these problems?

We shall wrestle with this question in the remaining chapters. But at this point let us consider an economy that places care needs first rather than last on its list of priorities, and which only then addresses the scope of production. In principle at least, such an economy, which places income and consumption levels at the disposal of care needs, will avoid causing today's now endemic problems to worsen. Such a reversal of priorities will reverse the direction of influence in the economy, so that the elements on the top half of the diagram come under the influence of the care required by the elements on the bottom half. We may call such an economy a "precare" economy. Our present economy is a "postcare" economy; in it we engage in the highest possible consumption and production and only afterwards attempt to mitigate the mounting care needs, often with extremely expensive forms of compensation.

Placing income and consumption levels at the disposal of care needs cuts to the heart of the *economics of enough*. In it a society or parts of a society instrumentally adopt income and employment levels (and with them, indirectly, production and consumption levels) in such a

63

way that they serve the objectives of providing sufficient care for human subsistence needs, the quality of labor, the sustainability of agricultural and urban ecosystems, and improved development opportunities, especially for the poorest countries of the Third World. Because all of these objectives identify fields of labor, labor that is both productive and transductive, implementing the economics of enough would also mean an end to the labor paradox. For where average income levels, including income levels in the directly productive sector, no longer rise, there we have cleared a path for directing the resulting economic surplus toward the care activities required. And this will have the effect of no longer endangering the current volume of transductive labor.

CHAPTER 3

Reclaiming People and Their Needs

Let us now take stock of the economic paradigm operative in our society today, and then attempt to contribute to its renewal.

By and large, reports on the course of a nation's economic life today render judgments solely on the basis of quantitative givens. Driving the assessment of these givens is the commonly held assumption in our culture that higher growth is good, and higher growth than ever before is better. Conversely, a decline in growth implies that someone has made a mistake somewhere. And for a country that has boasted high growth figures for a number of years, lower growth is a sign of stagnation.

This growth premise appears to hold not just for national economies but also for industry. Industry considers more return than in the past year good; it views less return as bad, and a poor return causes the stock market to become nervous. With virtually no exception, industry equates the lowering of costs with improved efficiency, and if a company can produce more with fewer employees, regardless of the consequences, then we consider the company a success.

All of this reflects the unmitigated power of growth thinking in our society. Again, we consider it better to grow by 3 percent than by 2.5 percent, because the extra growth allows us to do more. A sprinkling of politicians may suggest where they would like to earmark the surplus, if they could, but in most cases we assume that we shall spend the surplus on consumption. More consumption means more investment, and more investment means more production. This is growth, and this is progress.

If the growth paradigm is indeed so deeply rooted in our society, then this prompts a series of remarkable questions. First, have we derived any lessons from the events of the 1970s and 1980s? And secondly, what impact, if any, has the debate about economic renewal carried out between 1973 and 1980 had? During that period a series of compelling books and articles were published, criticizing the course of affairs in economic life, partly in reaction to the first oil crisis and partly in reaction to the reports of the Club of Rome. Stirring appeals for economic renewal came from Schumacher, Daly, Mishan, Scivorsky, Binswanger, Eppler, Hirsch, and many others.

Let us consider these questions in terms of the trio of economic problems described in Chapter 1. With respect to unemployment, the 1970s and 1980s demonstrated that a robust expansion of growth does not always bring employment levels back up to previous standards. Ironically, in most of the countries of the North, unemployment figures in the 1980s did *not* show a dramatic tendency to drop, despite the fervid economic growth of that period. Similarly, as we noted in Chapter 1, poverty in the Third World became structurally entrenched precisely during the 1970s and 1980s. Likewise, the increased production of the 1970s and 1980s brought heavy pressure on the environment, which significantly contributed to the environmental crisis flagged in Chapter 1.

It is striking, then, that despite the damage done to ourselves, others, and the environment, our approach to economic life appears to have emerged unscathed. How is it that in the face of this damage we appear to have ignored any potential lessons of the past two decades? Many people today tout a more vigorous increase in production as the solution to the unemployment crisis today. Indeed, they often do so with a greater sense of urgency than ever before. Similarly, except for discussions under way in a few sectors of industry, today's debate does not entertain the issue of the quality of work. In terms of poverty, our attention to the poor gradually flagged during the 1970s and 1980s. And to the extent that we now devote attention to poverty in the Third World and within our society, we still work with the concepts of the seventies. Finally, the increased production recommended for creating jobs will bring more and more pressure on the environment, certainly when unaccompanied by special measures and attention. Today's commonly accepted argument that we must "earn" more money through more production so that we can fund improvements to the environment puts the cart before the horse. Indeed, it brings to mind the plan suggested during the 1970s to preserve the environment by building higher smokestacks.

At the same time, the debate about economic renewal appears to have become derailed. During the years 1980 to 1983, the stagnation and partial economic decline begun in the late 1970s (partly due to the second oil crisis) demanded almost all of the attention, despite the series of compelling books and articles urging the renewal of the economy, and despite a good beginning in the public debate in the previous decade. In most industrialized countries discussions about government deficits, unemployment, and the system of social assistance accompanied debates about economic stagnation. Regrettably, during this later period the number of articles and books written about *renewing* the economy declined sharply. As far as we can determine, in terms of the problems identified in Chapter 1, the need to care for the environment occupied the most attention in the early 1980s as, influenced by huge cost increases, industrial energy consumption dropped. And throughout the past two decades we have continued to use the gross national product to measure growth and recession, in both absolute and relative terms.

In the early 1980s the authors of this book participated in a series of discussions with the chief executive officers of several Dutch transnational corporations, discussions that took place on behalf of the Dutch Council of Churches and at the request of the World Council of Churches.[1] What struck us in these conversations was that, against the backdrop of the events of the 1970s, the business leaders held to an unshaken faith in the need to grow. Likewise, they consistently maintained that growth — meaning a growth in production — was a condition for solving the problems of poverty, the environment, and unemployment. In other words, we saw no trace of the business community having a sense of social responsibility that would compel them to set the course of economic life toward meeting basic human need, thereby ameliorating violence. We also discovered no application of the discussion carried on over several years about the social costs

---

1. These discussions, together with commentary, were published in a book entitled *Over de grenzen: de maatschappelijke verantwoordelijkheid van transnationale ondernemingen* [Over the Limits: The Social Responsibility of Transnational Corporations] (Voorburg, 1984).

of production. For this they pointed us to the government, though at the same time they told us that by and large industry lobbied against current environmental regulations. They stated that usually industry considered them unnecessary and almost always too expensive.

Unfortunately, the chief executive officers of the transnational corporations do not form the exception. Politicians, too, today display very little consciousness of the debate about the need to fundamentally renew the economy or recognize the limits of growth. The old locomotive still stands on the rails, and many are busy trying to bring it up to speed. While in theory many acknowledge the presence of *new* scarcities, such as air, water, and time, they do not show signs of this awareness in practice.

None of this, however, is to say that many people do not hold lingering doubts about our society's approach to economic realities or that we do not understand the desire to walk in the footprints of old and antiquated ways. Doubts have indeed surfaced. But how far do these doubts reach? Will mere adjustments of economic policies and reformulations of the *known* pattern of economic ends and means be enough? Or must we perhaps dig deeper and reflect on an entirely different style of economic life?

Renewing Our Society's Economic Paradigm

Chapter 2 has supplied us with many arguments for reflecting on a new style of economic life. There we found that the science of economics has undergone a massive process of reduction in an effort to become objective and value free. As a beginning, ought not then the science of economics, as a partner in our society's overall economic orientation, to entertain the possibility of a "paradigm shift"? Ought not economists to return to deliberating about the foundations of our society in their work? They would not find themselves alone in such a self-examination. A number of scientists from a wide range of sciences have embarked on "paradigm discussions," in which they define "paradigm" as the intellectual model used to interpret reality and to discover practical ways of action. As a beginning, economists might ask themselves precisely *what* they want to pursue. For since World War II, they have asked primarily only *how* things happen.

Consider, for a moment, the irony of this request. For traditionally the science of economics has maintained that its object is *people and their needs*. Have not economists, then, in an effort to make themselves irreproachable as scientists, perhaps gradually strayed from the basic premise of economic science itself?

The answer to this question must include the observation that, with the postwar "mixed economy" and the erection of the welfare state, economists themselves attempted to soften several of the harsh sides of their own neoclassical framework. By means of the mixed economy, they have attempted to correct a number of the harrowing consequences of their own economic paradigm, the consequences we identified in Chapter 1. In some respects this development has been positive. The mixed economy encouraged economists to include the theory of political economy as a new subdivision of economics, and welfare economics brought with it the insight that we cannot view growth and accumulation as the most effective means for combating unemployment in every situation. It likewise led economists to subject the idea of consumer sovereignty to criticism. It generated economists' interest in the distribution of wealth, and it contributed to the insight that redistribution could help to increase the total prosperity of a country. With it, too, arose a willingness by economists to develop a budget mechanism alongside the market mechanism, to recognize the need to provide adequate care for people and then to integrate this into policy.

Regrettably, however, when viewed against the backdrop of the economic and cultural crises of our time, these modifications have not gone far enough. For in its foundations, as we saw in Chapter 2, current economic theory still remains incapable of addressing the root causes of poverty, environmental damage, unemployment, and the diminishing quality of work. It also has not and cannot adequately address the effects of economic activities on social and political structures. It cannot reverse our abandonment of the role of intermediary institutions and the resulting concentration of power, nor can it speak to our cleavage of the relationship between people and nature. Finally, it cannot address the dominance of the market mechanism as the means for solving problems in the local and world economy.

Our ultimate goal, then, is that a renewed ethic of economic responsibility gain acceptance within the whole of society. We shall argue for an ethic of responsibility, an ethic that therefore seeks to pursue the interests of *others* rather than self-interest. As the heart of this ethic, we turn to the scriptural command to love God and our neighbor, a command that stands at the center of the gospel. Love of God and neighbor seeks justice; it knows the difference between justice and injustice. Thus it is from this perspective that we seek to contribute toward defining a new and renewed notion of economic responsibility and a renewed economic paradigm.

Economic science has always said that it wants to orient itself to *people and their needs.* Given what we have observed in Chapters 1 and 2, has not economic science today then perhaps left its moorings? And ought not society and our culture as a whole to adopt this maxim as a starting point for its renewed economic paradigm?

But if society adopts this classical economic maxim, then clearly it cannot mean *some* people and their needs, even if these people number several hundred million. Nor can it mean satisfying the material desires of several hundred million people without paying attention to the basic subsistence needs of future generations. We must, in other words, locate an economic paradigm that incorporates the needs of *all.* Our society cannot accept economic science's reductionist battering of its original premise. Instead, our society must frame a renewed interpretation of the old economic maxim, an interpretation rooted in the desire to meet the needs of the other.

Orienting ourselves to the needs of the other leads us to define three dimensions of a renewed economic paradigm. We propose that in today's context our society accept as its first priority (1) meeting the needs of the *poor;* (2) reorienting the priorities of the *rich;* and (3) giving due weight to the needs of *future generations.*

The Poor

As we saw in Chapter 2, concern for the poor is not just a matter of ethics. It is an issue that, when economics has been defined rigorously and consistently, belongs to economics itself. Because any approach is unreliable if it does not take seriously its own premise (in this case, care for people and their needs), the needs of the poor properly belong to economic life itself, even if the market mechanism cannot register their needs. In this context, our current predilection for satisfying the material desires of people living in the Northern Hemisphere creates a dilemma. It is the dilemma that surfaces in everyone's life at the point at which meeting basic subsistence needs crosses over into the territory of satisfying material desires. And increasingly in our time meeting our material luxury needs *preempts* the possibility of meeting the genuine economic needs of others. As a society we must now confront this dilemma head on. We must also focus on the economic differentials dividing various groups of people, including those people who are entitled to financial assistance. Naturally, all of this also has significant ramifications for the science of economics itself.

Our society must therefore focus its lens on the poor. We think of those who live at or below poverty levels — of those, in other words, who live in life and death circumstances, such as the children who die each day because of starvation and exhaustion. Those who live in affluent countries often find it difficult to imagine the oppressive grip of poverty. But consider again the heart of a renewed ethic of economic responsibility, namely, the injunction to love God and our neighbor. In the gospel, Jesus announces freedom to the poor. The German theologian Jürgen Moltmann writes about the poor:

> The poverty meant [by Matthew and Luke] extends from economic, social and physical poverty to psychological, moral and religious poverty. The poor are all those who have to endure acts of violence and injustice without being able to defend themselves. The poor are all who have to exist physically and spiritually on the fringe of death, who have nothing to live for and to whom life has nothing to offer. The poor are all who are at the mercy of others, and who live with empty and open hands. Poverty therefore means both dependency and openness. We ought not to confine "poverty" in religious terms to the general dependence on God. But it cannot be interpreted in a merely economic or physical sense either. It is an expression which describes the enslavement and dehumanization of man in more than one dimension. The opposite of the poor in the Old Testament is the man of violence who oppresses the poor, forces them into poverty and enriches himself at their expense.[2]

Information from the world of the poor itself shows that in increasing measure they are becoming conscious of their situation.

2. Jürgen Moltmann, *The Church in the Power of the Spirit* (New York: Harper & Row, 1980), 79.

They have always known that they are poor. But now they also know why they are poor. It has been shown many times that historically the perpetuation of poverty is associated partly with efforts to convince the poor that they will gain a future reward for their poverty, and it is striking that gradually this, too, is now changing. If earlier the poor simply accepted their fate, now they are understanding in increasing fashion that their poverty is the result of an economic and social order adopted by others, an order that has the potential to be changed. They have set submission and passivity aside. In some regions a Marxist vision feeds this process; in other regions a Christian vision has brought inspiration and renewal.

In a number of Latin American countries the poor have found that the biblical stories contain their story. They have recognized themselves in the biblical stories and are actively drawing out the consequences. This in turn confronts the rich in the developed countries with a challenge, a challenge that in our view we in the North have not yet sufficiently taken up. Proposals framed by the World Council of Churches, the Catholic Church, and other church bodies to take steps toward solidarity with the poor have thus far remained unanswered. Our impression remains that the theological community of the developed countries still does not allow sufficient room for the Christian faith experiences of people from other cultures and races. And until this happens, theology in the developed world will not be genuinely ecumenical.

Nevertheless, the ecumenical movement has strongly encouraged the pathos for public justice. Public justice is linked inextricably with a biblical understanding of God. The South African theologian Allan Boesak dynamically voices this understanding when he writes, "God is glorified when the hungry are fed, the naked clothed, and the homeless are given shelter. God is glorified when children are able to grow into healthy adults and God is glorified when we use our resources to fight poverty, seek justice and love peace."[3]

This concept of public justice helps to give some content to the renewed paradigm and economic practice that the reclamation of the classical maxim demands. It suggests that in a society those needs that

---

3. Allan Boesak, "God van de armen" [God of the Poor], in *Met de Moed der Hoop, Opstellen Aangeboden aan dr. C. F. Beyers Naudé* [Encouraged by Hope: Essays Dedicated to Dr. C. F. Beyers Naudé] (Baarn: Bosch, Baarn en Keuning, 1985), 73.

make life possible and that preserve life must take priority. In terms of the actions of the rich, it calls them to adopt the principle of restitution: the return of possessions to their original owners. This is how we understand the story of the Year of Jubilee (Deuteronomy 15; Leviticus 25) and its reemphasis throughout the whole of the Scriptures. With this story, the fulfillment of which Jesus adopts as his mandate on earth (Luke 4:18-21), God announces freedom from want and fear to *all*.

The Rich

We are aware that all of this has serious consequences for those who live in Western society. It means, for example, transforming our current understanding of "stewardship" and "charity." We must not merely ask the question of what to do with our money, but we must raise the prior, more fundamental question: "How did I receive the money I have?" The church itself must provide an answer to this question, because behind it lies the reality that wealth has accumulated in the hands of a few, while the majority of God's people on earth die of hunger and misery. The church must further entertain the prospect of change. In the light of those people whose very lives are immediately threatened, the church must set aside the fear and trembling that shackle us in the face of the unknown, and it must begin to change. For immediate threat to life is a daily reality for hundreds of millions of people living in the developing countries.

People will show more inclination for change when they realize that present economic certainties are illusory. To the degree that information about poverty and chronic environmental abuse improves, to the degree that people perceive how fragile their own economic course is and how disadvantageous the growing economic differentials within their own societies are, perhaps then people will understand the illusions lurking behind our present economic activity.

All of this then raises this central question: How do we renew the economy so that a broader perspective can emerge within it for the poor? We must begin by defending the perspective that we have already acquired and that often comes under attack during difficult economic times. We must, for example, fight the fallacy that economic growth by definition is an adequate remedy for poverty or unemployment. We must argue the case that though increased military expenditures do lead to a growth in production and employment, such growth may be economically fatal. We must promote the notion that when we simply apply the market mechanism, invariably the unused productive forces orient themselves to those with the highest incomes. In sum, we must urge our society to renew its outmoded economic approach so that alleviating poverty becomes paramount.

But then we must define basic economic principles. And in today's context, broad ethical principles, such as alleviating suffering, meeting need, combating injustice, and reducing violence, suggest such a basic economic principle. Our Western society must accept a *minimal provision for our own basic needs (as well as for the basic needs of all)*, in conjunction with establishing a *maximum level of consumption*.

Let us consider, by way of two examples, the principle of accepting a minimal rather than an excessive provision for our needs in the West. Today much of the provision for our own food needs is excessive and has harmful effects. A United Nations report shows that in the rich nations the indirect consumption of grain in the form of meat and dairy products has reached such a scale that it causes human health to suffer. Along with this, in all of the rich countries "prosperity diseases," or food-related and other diseases caused by a rising standard of living, have driven up the costs of health care. In these same countries a significant squandering of food also occurs. To make matters worse, as Wendell Berry has eloquently noted time and time again, the astonishingly high food production of the affluent nations increasingly occurs at the expense of the sustainability of the land and of agricultural communities. In *What Are People For?* Berry writes that this productivity "is based on the ruin both of the producers and the source of production."[4] The food industry itself shows little interest in these problems, and most people have yet to resist the advertising that hawks the "new" products produced by the industrial food producers. The majority of industrial food producers in the West today use "more and more" rather than "enough" as their catchphrase, despite the reality that we live in an age of overconsumption and pay a heavy price for it.

But let us assume for a moment, as Berry's title implies, that people are not made for production, but production for people.

4. Wendell Berry, *What Are People For?* (San Francisco: North Point Press, 1990), 124.

Adopting this as our directive, we must then implement the concept of "enough" in the food sector. For the sake of the poor, the sustainability of agricultural ecosystems and communities, the deterioration of our health, and burgeoning health care costs, we must pursue a *sufficient* or minimal level of provision for our food needs.

A second example comes from the field of energy. An avalanche of literature has shown that our sloppy handling and overconsumption of energy form a serious threat to the environment and to the ability of future generations to provide for their own needs. Though the energy "experts" consider the development of alternative energy sources impossible, and not just because of the costs, recently work has surged on developing alternative energy sources. Despite little investment and incentive, the number of solar, wind, and other forms of power applications rise each year. For example, Toronto's renowned Hugh McMillan Rehabilitation Centre, an eighty-six-bed hospital for children with disabilities, is currently in the process of installing a one-hundred kilowatt solar cell photovoltaic array, 25 percent of which is already in operation.[5] In Sacramento, California, the municipal utility operates a massive one-megawatt photovoltaic array adjacent to the Rando Seco nuclear power plant, the first stage of a one-hundred megawatt solar cell power plant.[6] And according to a recent *Washington Times* report, a technical breakthrough in solar cell design makes possible a cost projection for the production of electricity with solar cells that matches the cost of electricity produced by fossil fuels today.[7] Similarly, wind-generated power already is "surprisingly competitive."[8] These and other examples of the inroads made by new alternatives have significance, because they teach us that public priorities can help put the economic engine on track.

5. As reported in *SOL: The Voice of Renewable Energy in Canada* 90 (September-October 1992): 2. The project is a joint effort on the part of Ontario Hydro, the federal Ministry of Energy, Mines and Resources, and the Ontario Ministry of Energy.

6. As reported in Joel Davidson, *The New Solar Electric Home: The How-To Photovoltaic Handbook* (Ann Arbor, Mich.: AATEC Publications, 1990), 13. The author calls for a ten-year national effort toward research and application of photovoltaics, similar to the effort to land astronauts on the moon.

7. Michael Grätzel, "Low Cost Solar Cells," *The World and I* 8, no. 2 (February 1993): 228-35.

8. Al Gore, *Earth in the Balance* (New York: Houghton Mifflin Company, 1992), 330.

Conversely, developing a maximum standard of consumption is desirable for several reasons. The first is that pressing for a strategy to meet basic subsistence needs has no credibility if the wealthy countries themselves do not put the brakes on their own material desires. We cannot use the excuse that human needs are infinite. Such an assumption, regardless of its validity or lack of validity, is incapable of serving as a directive for responsible action. Secondly, by accepting a maximum standard of consumption, perhaps in the form of an income policy, industrialized societies will slow down the continual escalation of real incomes, which we drive up in order to "keep up with the Joneses." This will have the effect of easing performance pressures in the money economy as well as creating avenues by which to improve the quality of life in society. Thirdly, accepting a maximum standard of consumption creates room for implementing the principle of restitution mentioned earlier. Fourthly, discussing the desirability of a maximum standard of consumption can serve to highlight the negative aspects of our "consumption society."

Finally, as we discuss opting for a maximum standard of consumption, we must consider the relative poverty present in our own regions. In addition to the indications of burgeoning poverty within the industrialized nations highlighted in Chapter 1, consider that in the United States in 1991 there was a 26 percent increase over the previous year in requests for emergency food assistance across major U.S. cities, only 17 percent of which were met.[9] Clearly, then, we must realign the forces of production in such a way that, in addition to meeting the basic subsistence needs of the poor in the Third World, we meet the needs of these people in the North. For their needs, too, rank among genuine economic needs, not material luxury desires.

Future Generations

The issue of creating a strategy for establishing a maximum standard of consumption flushes out a weighty question. What form of economic growth is legitimate, and for whom do we need it? This introduces the third dimension of a renewed economic paradigm for

9. Bread for the World Institute on Hunger and Development, *Hunger 1993* (Washington, D.C., 1992), 11.

our society and culture. Is an economic growth possible today that does not harm the subsistence possibilities of future generations? Current economic activity gives virtually no account to the needs of future generations. At present, as we noted in Chapter 2, today's production and consumption have effects on future generations that the market does not register but that nevertheless are very real. Though environmental contamination occurs gradually, it is conceivable that in a few decades it will become irreversible. Aspects of the extraction and depletion of resources, both of raw materials and of the nonrenewable sources of material prosperity, also figure in here. Those who as yet have no voice, the unborn, will discover the harmful consequences of our ways of producing and consuming.

We submit that in a renewed economic paradigm no form of economic growth is legitimate that violates the limits of sustainability, either for the poor today or for future generations tomorrow. We violate these limits when we use raw materials for products whose value is dubious. We also violate them when, for the sake of consumption in lucrative markets, we convert agricultural and horticultural production to create nonfood products.

Self-Interest or the Interest of Others?

The plea for our society to adopt a renewed economic paradigm and practice assumes that change is possible. It also assumes that, to a certain extent, we can "guide" the economy, as it were, because clearly without some form of guidance we cannot expect the market mechanism to deliver a good outcome. By this we mean that without other measures the operation of the market mechanism will not promote the "humanization" of our society and culture. Who, then, will guide the economy, and on behalf of whom? We shall return to this delicate issue at a later point. But clearly democracies need new sources of inspiration here. And in view of the dominance that the economy enjoys over social life, renewing our society's economic paradigm means that we must develop a new public ethos and regauge today's values. We must also describe, by means of a broad public educational effort, what is involved and what is at stake.

In our opinion, a renewed economic paradigm must proceed from the assumption that people need to advance the interests of *others*. People must be willing to think inclusively. They must choose to be led by considerations other than self-interest, a principle that belongs inextricably to the thought patterns of our society's current economic paradigm. Economists and others still widely accept the thesis that in and of itself self-interest plays a positive role in motivating people to reach higher achievements. But unless they can see an immediate and direct benefit from a certain action, we question whether people act strictly out of self-interest in every respect. In view of what neoclassical theory calls the "external effects" (for example, the influence of production on the environment) of everyday economic activity over the intermediate and long term, we seriously question whether ultimately self-interest can play a positive role. Instead, it often seems to serve a negative purpose, for we display much selfishness, both individually and collectively. There is also much that we overlook and much that we do not know. The principle that the individual's pursuit of material prosperity generates "social harmony" creates a false optimism. Jeremy Bentham's old utilitarian maxim, which still drives today's economic paradigm — namely, that when we pursue "the greatest happiness for the greatest number" we will automatically create social harmony — has never been borne out in any society, at any time in history.

Herman Daly proposes an alternative to Jeremy Bentham's maxim, an alternative that we believe ought to lie at the heart of our society's renewed economic paradigm. Daly proposes that we pursue "sufficient per capita product for the greatest number over time."[10] He uses here a term that, as we have seen, a renewed economic paradigm will find reliable, namely, the term "sufficient" or "enough."

In contrast to the word "growth," the word "enough" defines for all of us a relationship with the poor. It likewise has significance for the question posed earlier in this chapter, namely, the question of where the boundary lies dividing material luxury desires from the legitimate economic needs of people today and of future generations. It helps to define the basic economic principles in today's Western context of a minimal provision for our needs and a maximum standard of consumption. But economics alone cannot answer the question of where the boundary lies dividing luxuries from necessities, for it is

---

10. Herman Daly, "The Ecological and Moral Necessity for Limiting Economic Growth," in Roger S. Shinn, ed., *Faith and Science in an Unjust World* (Geneva: WCC Publications, 1980), 217.

also a political and cultural question. It is a question that we must discuss as broadly as possible, and we must articulate an answer in policy. The context for this discussion is that rising production now appears to create new scarcities, such as those of air, water, and time. These scarcities arise because rising production in the overdeveloped West violates the limits of sustainability, limits that in our view we have already violated.

In summary, by promoting a new or renewed economic paradigm, we have sought to strip off the restrictions that have shackled economists over the last several decades. We emphatically reject the reductionist paradigm of the science of economics; instead, we urge society as a whole, including economists, to reclaim the original focus of economics, namely, *people and their needs.* We have done this because of the need to opt for *all people,* and in all respects. We advocate bringing the dynamic elements of real life back into our society's economic paradigm. When we do so, we find that real life supplies us with two new streams of information, streams flowing out of the lives of vast numbers of people living in poverty locally and in the Third World and of those belonging to future generations. These streams and the people they represent cry out for an altered economic practice rooted in a renewed economic paradigm.

CHAPTER 4

Renewing Our Economic Order

Let us consider where we have alighted along the way. In Chapter 1 we described the main economic problems facing the world today: mounting poverty, the deterioration of the environment, and the loss of meaningful employment. In Chapter 2 we suggested that a relationship exists among these problems. In one way or another they all have to do with "calculations" implemented by society, calculations that no longer seem to add up. We saw that the science of economics actively participated in drafting these calculations, including those designed to solve poverty, environmental degeneration, and unemployment. The science of economics formulated them in terms of market, profit, labor, and growth, but never in terms of the need for the caring administration of what has been entrusted to us, which is the meaning of the word *economics.* That brought us in Chapter 3 to explore whether we might locate another economic paradigm for our society as a whole, and we arrived at an economics that takes as its first priority the real needs of people — an economics of the poor and of the carrying capacity of our environment to sustain the lives of future generations. We have alighted, in other words, on an economy of *precare,* an economy that places care needs first on its list of priorities, and only then addresses the scope of production.

Having said all of this, however, the problems described in Chapter 1 recoil upon us like a boomerang. For how, inspired by a different approach, can we alter today's full-fledged *postcare* economic and political practice? This practice is entirely pervaded by calculations built on money, growth, and the market, and only after the pursuit of these do we seek to alleviate the mounting care needs. The question itself may sound presumptuous, because people may not actually desire a different economic practice. A certain need has developed in our society to make calculations as we do now, and not differently. For not only have our economic calculations become embedded within our habits and traditions, but they have also been incorporated into the societal *order* or *structure* in which all of us live and move and have our being. Consider, for example, a business that attempts to convert on its own to providing more care for the environment, improving the quality of work, and retaining as many jobs as possible. It will quickly price itself out of the market and go bankrupt, simply because of the costs involved. This reality shows that when we seek to redress poverty, environmental degeneration, and unemployment we brush up against nothing less than the powerful influence of a societal *order*, an order whose signature is *progress measured in money*. And societal orders or structures do not easily surrender to change, as we see now again during Eastern Europe's difficult transition from a planned to a market economy.

Lessons from the Present

In this light, how realistic is it to expect that our current economic order can actually change? To a large degree, the answer to this question hinges on how we assess the significant events of our recent past, especially the fall of the Iron Curtain and the subsequent emergence of the Gulf Crisis. Specifically, do we understand these events as a sign of the *strength* or of the *weakness* of our own economic and political systems? For if we understand them simply as signs of strength, then we may have no reason or desire to pursue or expect change.

A current interpretation of what caused the Gulf War is that the entire international community of nations had a compelling interest in denouncing as quickly as possible any violation of human rights and of the principle of self-determination (in this case, the self-determination of Kuwait). If we accept this approach, then we interpret the Gulf Crisis as a sign of the *strength* of the international community of nations in general, and of the leading states, such as the United States, in particular. A parallel interpretation of the fall of the Berlin Wall understands it as a sign of the inner strength of Western society and of its dominant economic system. After all, our system lives on, but the planned economy collapsed before our very eyes! From this vantage point, both incidents affirm the order of society as we now know it, while in the European context they serve as the success formula by which to chart the future of Europe after its economic unification.

In Chapter 1, however, when discussing the causes of the Gulf Crisis, we proposed a somewhat different interpretation of the Gulf War. The fact that the rich nations had to intervene so quickly in a place where, at most, a *regional* conflict had flared up had a great deal to do with those nations' economic practice of walking in dangerously oversized shoes. The United States ranks second among the world's largest oil producers, but its own oil production cannot match its own much *larger* oil consumption, which ranks first in the world. Therefore, when the assurance of ongoing massive energy imports flagged, the United States reacted as if it had been stung. Did not former United States President Bush, echoing a statement he made at the beginning of the confrontation, declare at the 1992 Republican National Convention that the "decision to confront Saddam Hussein . . . assured the continued flow of oil to the rest of the world"?[1] The Gulf War then also reveals a fundamental *weakness* inherent in a superstate's enormous exercise of power: those who wish to walk in oversized shoes become treacherously dependent upon others. When Saddam Hussein invaded Kuwait, he touched the Achilles' heel not only of a political superpower but also of a highly dependent Western economic order.

The fall of the Iron Curtain also requires a second reading. This reading begins by raising the sober question of why the centrally planned economy was a failure. It begins, in other words, when we examine the planned economy as an economic system as such, not just as a weapon for securing the regime of a political/military dictatorship bent on terror and destruction.

There are many reasons why the centrally planned economy was a failure, reasons that all played a role in the collapse of the planned economies behind the Iron Curtain. Some have to do with how a single central plan operated in a complex economy that had long lines of command: it struggled through an enormous amount of bureaucracy and corruption, glaring inefficiency in production, and tremendous wasting of soil and energy through the most unrealistic

1. As reported in the *Toronto Star*, 21 August 1992, 23.

forms of price setting. But there are also other significant factors. In a planned economy, any economic plan, however decentrally applied and expertly implemented, is plagued with a number of built-in limitations. Specifically, in a planned economy each plan must have a *quantitative* slant; that is, each plan must be formulated solely in terms of prices and quantities. Further, in a planned economy each plan, no matter how short- or long-term, is able to approach the future only as if it were an extension of the present. In other words, the goals and projections of the plan rely solely on what is known about the present and the present state of affairs.

It was no accident, then, that the planned economies behind the Iron Curtain were full of crippling flaws. These flaws came to light when external shocks struck that fell outside of the frame of reference of the plan and when the quality of the environment and of society as a whole entered the picture, for no plan could entertain *non-quantitative* realities. And as one might expect, figures that described the present state of affairs often formed highly unreliable descriptions of the future.

Such assessments of the structural flaws of the planned economy are highly useful, because these basic flaws do not afflict only the operation of a central plan. Indeed, the institution of the *market* is plagued with similar flaws! For like the planned economy, the market economy requires an exclusively quantitative slant. As we saw in Chapter 2, in a pure market economy nothing has value unless it has a price. Although one might assume that culture, nature, and human health have substantial value, from the vantage point of the market they have no value: the market uses and employs them at no cost (at least as long as the government does not come in between). Further, the market cannot identify needs unless people lay money on the table, and without a financial return it cannot organize production processes to create supply. Of course, one cannot level this criticism at the institution of the market itself, because the market cannot help but be merely a world of money, prices, and quantities. Yet the quantitative limitations of the market *become* extremely dangerous when a society no longer acknowledges them, as occurs when a society uses the market as its ultimate compass. This is an example of what Daly and Cobb have called the "failure of misplaced concreteness."[2]

2. Herman E. Daly and John B. Cobb, *For the Common Good* (Boston: Beacon Press, 1989), 44.

Similarly, the very flaw that threatened the sustainability of life for future generations under the centrally planned economy plagues the market economy. Nobel prize–winning economist Jan Tinbergen has shown that in a market economy long-term scarcities have no influence on the prices of today. Because markets have a "time horizon" of no longer than eight to ten years, in a certain sense they are blind to the future.

This sober diagnosis shows that we cannot simply interpret the collapse of the planned economies in our time as a sign of the strength of what presents itself as the sole remaining alternative: the pure or mixed market economy. On the contrary, the planned economies' collapse also is a sign of the *weakness* of the market economy. For sooner or later the defects that tripped up the planned economies will cause the market economy to stumble, and for precisely the same reasons. For *both* the planned and the market economies are oblivious to that which is nonmaterial and nonquantitative, and *both* remain oblivious to the future.

In truth, the collapse of the Iron Curtain demonstrates that eternal life has not been granted to any economic order, whether that order be the planned or the market economy.

Three Areas of Societal Reorientation

Of course, recognizing that our present economic system may well fail over time, particularly if we are unwilling to alter it, does not in and of itself create a better or more sustainable alternative. It does, however, throw a different light on the conviction that change is neither possible nor desirable. For now it seems meaningful at least to consider what steps our society must take and what obstacles it must overcome to become a society of caring administration, a society that permits the development of a sustainable economy. In this chapter we shall identify three hurdles to cross, or three areas where society must reorient itself in its structure if it is to renew today's economy. They are the hurdles of (1) prioritizing and limiting our society's *ends;* (2) organizing and applying the *means* required to meet these ends; and (3) distributing and using economic *power* and *influence* to support these reorientations.

84

Economic Ends

First, to implement an economics of caring administration, our society must alter its approach to economic ends. Specifically, we must redefine the consumption goals served by our production system. Building on our paradigm discussion in Chapter 3, we may distinguish between three types of economic ends: (1) material luxury needs that are either harmful or frivolous; (2) needs that are real and significant but not essential to the preservation of life; and (3) basic subsistence needs. From this rough and necessarily somewhat arbitrary categorization we may tease out an ordering principle for any economy, especially an economy such as ours that operates in a world where untold human needs continue to remain unmet. This ordering principle is that, at the very least, basic subsistence needs (3) must take priority over luxury needs (1). More precisely, instead of using ethical categories such as "right" or "wrong," we must state that luxury needs tend to become *uneconomic* (that is, detrimental to the caring administration of what has been entrusted to us) when we satisfy them at the expense of meeting the basic needs of others.

Clearly, under this definition, the growth of material consumptive desires in contemporary North America, Western Europe, and Japan has tended and is tending to become more and more uneconomic. Not much discernment is needed to recognize that our desire to become wealthier in the North directly competes with efforts to meet subsistence needs in the South. For to satisfy our luxury needs we extract and use up the scarce soil, nonrenewable resources, and environmental capacity of the South that are required to meet the subsistence needs of the South.

But how can this global competition between the luxury needs of the North and the basic subsistence needs of the South ever subside? Obviously, more is involved than only national economic systems: here we encounter the influence of today's international economic order, or more precisely, of today's international monetary order. For acquiring higher levels of consumption and a higher standard of living depends on having access to currency that is acceptable in the international exchange.

To assess the prospect of change in the international monetary order, let us begin with the simple fact that if international trade is to continue to increase, then it can do so only if the quantity of international currencies available also increases. Otherwise enormous global deflation, or an enormous drop in world prices, would occur. But how are the growth and the manner of growth of international liquidities determined in today's world? Clearly, not every currency can grow in volume in order to prop up further increases in world trade. In fact, it is only those currencies that are accepted in international trade whose volume can increase. These are the so-called key currencies: the Japanese yen, the British pound, the Swiss franc, the German mark, and, in particular, the American dollar.

Bear in mind that if one's own monetary unit serves as an accepted means of payment in international trade, then one's own country has a relative economic advantage. This advantage, known as *seignorage,* consists of the difference between the actual costs of making the money and the value that the money possesses on the international exchange (just as earlier in history the value of a coin rose when a lord, a *seigneur,* validated it and permitted his image to be engraved upon it). The United States, as holder of the most important key currency today, has profited the most from the *seignorage* advantage. In the 1960s the United States was able to invest enormous amounts of money in Latin America and Europe, not to mention in the Vietnam war effort, though in doing so it also had to sustain substantial losses in gold. In 1971, however, the Nixon administration eliminated the practice of exchanging dollars for gold. The *seignorage* advantage then became crystal clear. For severing the tie between dollars and gold permitted the United States to maintain and increase its already high level of consumption by means of an almost permanent deficit in its balance of payments. At the same time, those countries that were not permitted to generate their own international liquidities, particularly Third World countries, found it increasingly difficult to hold their heads above water.

The history of the world money supply in the 1970s and 1980s graphically illustrates this converse relationship. Between 1969 and 1972, or in a period of no more than four years, the rich nations generated more international currencies than in the entire history of the world until 1969! Robert Triffin, who has described this phenomenon in his essay "Gold and the Dollar Crisis," notes that over 95 percent of this increase in currency came from and accrued to the wealthy countries themselves.[3] As one might expect, the value of these

3. Robert Triffin, "Gold and the Dollar Crisis: Yesterday and Tomorrow," *Essays in International Finance* 132 (December 1978).

currencies (that is, the price they received in the international exchange), especially that of the dollar, dropped as a result. And in 1973, reacting to the fact that they were receiving less and less valuable dollars for the oil that they exported, several oil-producing countries formed the OPEC bloc and tripled their oil prices, resulting in the first "oil crisis."[4]

It is critical to observe that it was the poorest countries of the world — sometimes called the NOPEC countries because, in addition to their poverty, they lack their own energy resources — that bore the full blow of the oil crisis, a blow that had much greater force than all of the development aid granted to them after World War II. Lacking the opportunity to generate their own international currencies, they had no choice but to borrow money in order to import the oil that had now become instantly more expensive. Remarkably, precisely at this time borrowing money was a genuine possibility for them, and even at low interest rates. For did not the wealthy nations and their banks possess an oversupply of currency?

Tragically, this crossroads also marks the beginning of the unbelievable rise in the burden of debt of the world's poor countries during the 1970s and 1980s. For later, when interest rates rose sharply in 1979, the poor countries could not meet their loan payment obligations and therefore had no choice but to borrow again — this time at interest rates that, as we have noted, averaged no less than 17 percent (in real terms) in the 1980s. This in turn led to the current reverse net transfer from the South to the North, which by 1991 had escalated to an amount of $50 billion annually.

4. As described in *Idols of Our Time,* the Western nations reacted in three ways to the oil crisis. First, they made new money! In the next three years, from 1972 to 1975, world money reserves doubled (Robert Triffin, "Gold and the Dollar Crisis," 4). Second, they borrowed enormous sums of money from the oil countries, which had become instantly rich. And third, they increased exports, largely from the most technologically advanced sector of the economy: weapons production. In one year, from 1973 to 1974, the weapons exports of the United States doubled from $4 billion to $8 billion, thereby raising the weapons ceiling in the world as a whole. The combined effect of these reactions led to the second energy crisis of 1978, a crisis that skewed the Western balance of payments even more seriously than the first. For from 1978 on, the repeated shock therapy essentially decelerated Western economic growth, as the burden of debt and government deficits in the West reached hitherto unknown heights (Bob Goudzwaard, *Idols of Our Time,* trans. Mark R. Vander Vennen [Downers Grove, Ill.: InterVarsity Press, 1984], 88-91).

We therefore conclude that the reverse net transfer is not an accident. Rather, it is the outcome of the highly inequitable structure of our international monetary order. That order permits *wealthy* debtor nations, such as the United States (the largest debtor nation in the world), to finance ongoing increases in their standard of living with virtually no restriction. But it requires *poor* debtor nations constantly to "adapt" their economies in order to meet their debt obligations. This deep inequity violates not only the rule of justice but also the rule of good economy. For by means of this inequity we satisfy luxury needs at the expense of meeting basic subsistence needs.

So it is that the flip side of the rising material prosperity of the North is the rising indebtedness of the South during the 1970s and 1980s. Meanwhile, the rising material prosperity of the North is made possible by a built-in imbalance in the world monetary system that grants the wealthy nations untrammeled access to the world's money spigots but that refuses the same access to the poor nations. Yet acknowledging this reality may open up prospects for finding a way to limit access to the creation of international liquidities to the rich nations but to increase such access to the poor nations. A step such as this could serve as a decisive contribution to an economically improved distribution of income and consumption around the world.

There is a final respect in which the issue of altering our economic ends brushes up against the economic order or structure of our society. In an economy of care, economic needs or ends include more than what the output of production processes can satisfy. They also include what human *culture* needs to survive: a minimum level of care for the sustainability of the environment, so that it will remain fertile; a minimum level of care for the sustainability of human communities, so that people's care for each other will acquire continuity and tradition; and a minimum level of care for employment opportunities and the quality of work. Because these elements of care also rank among genuine economic needs, satisfying people's rising luxury needs may not run roughshod over these genuine basic economic needs.

We may therefore describe the first obstacle in this manner: in its structuring, our industrialized society must include certain qualitative needs, such as the sustainability of the environment and of human communities, among basic subsistence needs, and then give all basic needs priority over luxury needs.

88

Economic Means

With this redefinition of economic ends or needs, a unique problem surfaces. It would seem that realigning economic needs as we have done means that our production system must serve more needs than ever before. For not only must we meet the needs of the poor, but we must also satisfy the requirements of care: care for the environment, employment, and the quality of work. How then can we meet additional needs if our *means* have not expanded? And does not the expansion of our means require precisely what our postcare economic order urges, namely, economic growth?

This question brings us to the second obstacle that our society must overcome, or to the second fundamental change required. To become a society of caring administration, we must alter our structural approach to economic *means*.

Let us begin by taking the most direct approach to this obstacle. If we add improved care for the environment, employment, and the quality of work to our list of economic needs, then to a certain extent the problem solves itself. For these areas of need invite a sizable amount of employment. Though directing employment to these areas requires separate measures, in this respect there is no question of needing to expand our means in order to meet additional needs.

This does not yet describe the heart of the means issue, however. The predicament is this: it may seem that adopting an economy of care faces an insurmountable obstacle at the level of means. Every form of work brings with it the need for remuneration or wages of some kind, and wages bring with them the desire to spend more. But is there room for this in a society of caring administration? Have we not said that the desire to spend prevents us from meeting real needs in society?

This issue sheds light on the more complete alteration of economic means or resources required. While it may sound startling, it is inescapable: if we must, as suggested above, provide care for economic means (including the means of production) thereby giving them the status of economic needs or necessities, then conversely our society's level of material desires must now become "means" available for meeting our newly defined economic ends. In other words, *our society must invert its economic means and ends,* so that our ends (material desires) become serviceable as means for meeting genuine need. Put in another way, our society's standard of living must now become the variable in the economic model. And for this to occur, our society may no longer grant every material desire a place on its list of priorities.

Here lurks the painful heart of the "economics of enough." The economics of enough entails putting priority, in the very form we give to our economic order, on meeting economic *needs:* the needs of the poorest, of those looking for work, of the environment and its sustainability, and of human community. But this re-forming of our economic order comes at a price, a price that human material desires must pay. In an economics of enough, a society must be willing to accept that general income increases — across-the-board wage hikes — will gradually come to an end. Then, by using the moneys that this frees up to meet basic needs, we open the door to permitting genuine needs to enter our social scheme of priorities. Indeed, in principle we would ensure that these needs would be met.

Our second obstacle therefore is to make present-day economic ends instruments for meeting basic needs.

Linking Economic Ends and Means

Unfortunately, hurdling the obstacles of altering our approach to both economic ends and means does not yet complete the full reorientation required to renew today's economy. In order to be effective, our society must *link* its reorientation of needs and means. And the need for this linkage forms the third and final obstacle that our society must cross: we must alter the ways in which ends and means become connected in our society.

In smaller working communities the joining of needs to means does not create a serious obstacle. In them a rather spontaneous linkage arises connecting the needs and resources of the community. The kibbutz in Israel has provided a good example of this. The kibbutz is a democratic community where people live and work. Its members first jointly establish what tasks they must accomplish, tasks that the care requirements of the community define. Only then do they decide what means remain available for satisfying individual material desires. The priority that the kibbutz members first give to what is truly needed (including gathering and producing the community's provisions and ensuring that each person has work) serves as a natural limit

— though not always without tension — to the amount of income and consumption possible for community members.

A similar process occurs in cooperative businesses. In the Netherlands, for example, about two thousand small businesses called MEMO companies have sprung up. MEMO companies have adopted as their first priority to operate in such a way that they are environmentally friendly, energy saving, and socially responsible. In a MEMO company a fine attunement occurs between ends and means. Each company's goals lie firmly planted in caring for the environment, saving energy, and producing a responsible product, using the input of all of its members. The company is able to achieve this because its members have chosen to accept a lower income than they could earn elsewhere: in some cases, even minimum wage. But MEMO companies consciously cut the coat according to the size, pattern, and color of the cloth, in clear contrast to society at large, which does so according to the requirements not of the fabric but of maximum consumption.

However they may differ, we may consider kibbutzes and MEMO companies miniature economies of enough. For they demonstrate on a small scale how the primacy of care can function economically in a society.

But can we expect a similar spontaneous linkage of ends and means to occur in our society as a whole? No, we cannot. For people do not experience mutual support and encouragement in society at large. Further, we cannot expect this linkage to occur in industries, organizations, or unions whose objective is not to implement caring administration but to obtain maximum return or to win the highest possible salaries and benefits spread over the greatest number of years. In all of these contexts, if we are to connect needs and means in such a way that they permit the implementation of caring administration, then we must locate another manner of linkage. Here we face the issue of how to distribute and exercise economic power or control. In all of these contexts new channels must be dug to allow the flow of at least part of the buying power provided by net disposable income to meet the real care needs of society, wherever they may lie.

Let us first consider the microeconomic context. For people in various industries, organizations, and unions this conscious structural reallocation of buying power to meet genuine care needs seems to lie within the realm of possibility. It means that they must expand their goals to include demonstrating more care for employment, people, and the environment, in *combination* with a willingness to limit the income they would otherwise receive. This in turn presumes one of two things. It presumes renewing the manner by which control is exercised in industries, organizations, and unions, so that employees who allow portions of their incomes to "sit," as it were, naturally become full partners in making the decisions about how to allocate these moneys. Or it presumes that the social partners in the company or industrial sector settle on binding agreements that, in exchange for losses in income, include addressing the amount and type of jobs available. Recent precedents in North America and Europe of exchanging income for both jobs and the improvement of work quality signal a small beginning in this direction. By digging a new channel for buying power to flow through, all of those involved exercise economic control in the direction of preserving employment, not destroying it.

When it comes to society as a whole, however, the need to redirect buying power and reorient the exercise of economic control encounters significant barriers. For here we confront our economic order itself, an order that aims at precisely the *opposite* of what we have in mind! Our contemporary economic order systematically wields power and control in such a way that they support the continual increase of the outflow of goods and services and the incomes connected to this. As we saw earlier, this increase is also touted as a solution to the critical lack of attention given to all areas requiring care; it is partly motivated, in other words, by the postcare requirements of our economic order. Seeking to implement caring administration by limiting income and consumption growth therefore includes attempting to reverse the direction in which economic power is presently exercised in our society.

We may therefore expect that every attempt to modify our economic order toward adopting care as its primary objective will meet fierce resistance from those who now wield power, whether those modifications come by way of imposing care requirements on industries, requiring binding agreements on the use of responsible technologies, or establishing controls over wages and salaries through a more guided wage and salary policy. In reaction, people in power will appeal to the perception that we all *want* economic control exercised in such a manner that it increases productivity, or that at least all of us tacitly approve of it doing so, because all of us realize that every slowdown in the tempo of economic growth and technological development will cost us dearly in terms of maintaining and raising our standard of living.

This third area — the linkage of ends and means — therefore confronts us with our most unforgiving and seemingly irrevocable obstacle. Perhaps our only consolation is that at least this obstacle is not technological or organizational. Rather, it has to do with our *culture*, with our whole manner of life and of living in society. For when the chase of money and power form the trademark of a culture, as Tawney has described in his compelling book *The Acquisitive Society*, obviously such a culture will not produce the fine attunement needed between decreasing consumption and implementing care. Rather, that culture will continue to exercise control toward what we can get, obtain, and acquire. It will argue vehemently that without this our society will die. Did not former United States President Dwight Eisenhower, faced with the market backwash threatening American industries, explain in crystal clear terms, "It is the duty of every American to consume"?

In this light, how can we overcome this final obstacle of linking ends and means in such a way that they encourage the adoption of a precare economy, when the present exercise of economic power *itself* reinforces the priorities of our contemporary economic order?

Reasonable Doubt

Let us inspect this final obstacle closely, however. In reality, it is most peculiar. For it suggests that, at its most fundamental level, economic power operates as it does today because all of us who compulsively clutch and grab at material things authorize it to do so. The argument assumes or presupposes that, when it comes down to it, the vast majority of us would rather raise our material standard of living than give priority to caring for the poor, the environment, the unemployed, and the people around us. But is this actually true in all respects?

The answer to this question takes on extraordinary significance. For the degree to which such pure materialism does *not* accurately describe all of us is the degree to which this final hurdle might reveal a flaw, an opening, a kind of crack in the wall. And where walls have cracks, walls can come down. Is it conceivable, in and of itself, that an economic order such as ours can continue to revolve toward further economic expansion, even after such expansion no longer conforms to people's genuine desires?

Certainly it is conceivable. At least three arguments suggest that a disjuncture may exist between what people genuinely desire and what actually takes place in our economic order. They are the *flywheel, spoilsport,* and *magnifying glass* arguments.

The Flywheel

The flywheel argument refers to the physical phenomenon that when something is set in motion, it can keep spinning on its own for a long time. We have every reason to see our economic order as something that has been set in motion. "Capitalism," wrote the great economist Joseph Schumpeter, "is a form or matter of change." Its growth did not follow a biological pattern. Rather, it sprang up as a project of expanding the wealth of the nations at a time when poverty dominated Europe in many areas. Given its context, it is no wonder that capitalism became almost instantly popular. Capitalism made it possible for industries, as distinct from the earlier guilds, to place the lowering of costs and the expansion of sales among their primary goals, spurred on as they were by fierce, full-fledged competition — the new element in the economic order. But if a society has organized itself around this fundamental orientation toward increased growth and production, and if a substantial number of institutions have sprung up around it, then we cannot expect immediate change when that society begins to cast doubt upon its fundamental orientation or when each round of production growth increases material prosperity. For the *momentum* of the social order carries it on, while at the same time many forms of economic power still reinforce the growth orientation. In addition, our economic order has devised many built-in instruments for ensuring its self-preservation, such as endless advertising pressure. For if we are to assure the expansion of sales that makes possible the expansion of productivity, then the material desires of people must continually increase.

The flywheel argument therefore suggests that, like a flywheel that sets a system of gears in motion, our societal order can continue revolving even after its initial impetus has ceased.

The Spoilsport

The spoilsport argument relates to the circumstance that, even assuming that large groups of people would want to implement a different economic practice, we still could not throw the switch that would send the train down a different track. Almost nothing is as disheartening as when, individually or collectively, one obeys self-imposed economic restraints for the sake of protecting the environment or fighting poverty, while others quite consciously refuse to do the same and thus walk off with all the benefits. Economists call this the prisoners' dilemma.[5] In the philosophical problem of the prisoners' dilemma, each of two prisoners must weigh these choices: (1) if one confesses and implicates the other, who remains silent, the first goes free and the second gets a long prison sentence; (2) if both confess and implicate each other, both get moderate prison sentences; (3) if both remain silent, both get light prison sentences on another charge. It is to each prisoner's advantage to talk, but it is to their collective advantage to stay silent, and therein lies the dilemma.

Years ago Dutch economists Jan Tinbergen and Hans van den Doel used the prisoners' dilemma to demonstrate that voluntary wage and salary restraints will never succeed, even if everyone is convinced that things would actually improve as a result. For there are always people and groups of people who, taking stock of the situation, will spot a clear opportunity to sacrifice nothing but profit from the advantages. And who among us would grant others that chance, even if it is remote? It seems, then, that people will voluntarily moderate next to nothing. Wage moderation will succeed only where collectively agreed upon and/or where imposed from above. Without such leverage, the spoilsport spoils the possibility of implementing a responsible economic practice, even when the majority of people desire such a practice.

The Magnifying Glass

The magnifying glass argument is the most remarkable of the three, but also the most real. It is connected with the fact that countless

5. See Mancur Olson, *The Logic of Collective Action: Public Goods and the Theory of Groups* (Cambridge, Mass.: Harvard University Press, 1965).

people represent us as citizens at the decision-making levels of our society. The remark was once made that, when seen from government centers such as Washington, Ottawa, or London, a country's population appears to consist of at least ten times its actual number. For all of us are "members" of numerous public groupings — whether as citizens of a community or as members of various organizations, for example — each of which in some context lobbies government on our behalf. All of us therefore find ourselves represented in multiple ways. However, in nine out of ten cases our own material interests arrive at the decision-making levels of government, while perhaps in only one out of ten cases do our concerns for the protection of the environment or for meeting the needs of the poor reach these levels, and even then they do so only if we happen to belong to an organization or community for which these form a priority.

So it is that a "magnifying glass" of multiple representation enlarges the influence of our own material desires while, conversely, the single representation shrinks the influence of the real economic needs of people or things. Not much attention therefore comes from our national or international capitals to meet basic economic needs, in part because we ourselves send often entirely conflicting signals to the government. As a result, in spite of our good words and intentions, the heavy machinery grinds on, merely creating more and more for ourselves.

*   *   *

The arguments described above suggest three ways in which the momentum of our economic order may spin toward further economic expansion even if the majority of people no longer support that expansion. But do these arguments actually help? For they suggest that a possible disjuncture divorces people's genuine desires from the actual operation of our economic order. And does this not imply that the direction of our economic order lies outside our hands? Does this not render our situation far more bleak than we had imagined? Taken together, these three arguments may seem strong enough to put the chances of genuinely transforming our economic order at next to nil.

But we vigorously refute this conclusion. Consider this: if we trace these arguments again — the flywheel, spoilsport, and magnifying glass arguments — it is striking that not one of them roots its argument in the intrinsic goodness or enduring value of our contemporary economic order. And this suggests that, at minimum, no *necessary* relationship exists between what would genuinely serve human needs and what our economic order accepts as its directives.

This is already a significant insight. For it leads to two conclusions, which will occupy us in the next chapter.

First, we may not exclude the possibility that, although our economic order creates an impression of enormous vitality, under the surface it is no longer responsive to the cultural demands of our time. If this is the case, then our economic order may well be *internally out of date.* And secondly, to the degree that our economic order may be out of date, it will gradually lose its hold on our society sufficiently for us to find ways to alter it at its essential points.

CHAPTER 5

Revitalizing Our Outdated
Economic Order

In Chapter 4 we observed that a change of our economic order is at least conceivable. At the same time, the implementation of change in our society faces the hurdles of redefining our society's economic ends, making our society's means serviceable to these ends, and then linking these together and coordinating them. With the flywheel, spoilsport, and magnifying glass arguments, we also noted that the readiness for change in our society may well be more real than we might have assumed. We therefore ended by suggesting that under the surface our economic order may no longer be responsive to the cultural demands of our time; in other words, that it may well be *internally out of date.* And to the extent that our economic order is out of date, it will gradually lose its hold on our society sufficiently for us to find ways to alter it at its essential points.

We do not usually hear our vibrant Western economic order described as "internally out of date"! Yet at least three strong signals indicate that this profile is entirely appropriate.

Three Signals That Our Economic Order Is Outdated

The Industrial Paradox

First, a remarkable paradox has materialized in our time, a paradox that ties into both the care and labor paradoxes described in Chapter 1.

It is the industrial paradox. When the material prosperity of society increases, then economically we would expect that after some time industrial production would reach a kind of saturation point. We would expect that beyond a certain income level people would exert proportionately greater demand for nonmaterial services and provisions than for industrial products. In practice, however, we often see the *reverse:* industrial goods increasingly replace personal services. Service robots have begun to substitute for nurses in hospitals, computers and videos teach students as more and more teachers become unemployed, and compact discs are selling rapidly even as orchestras are forced to close their doors. This process of increasing industrialization is occurring at a rapid pace, and it is critical that we understand its cause.[1]

Perhaps its most important cause is simply that industrial products tend to become less expensive than many nonmaterial provisions and services. It is no wonder that they do: the law of decreasing costs applies to industrial products, because the introduction of cost-saving technologies in an environment of rising production allows market prices to remain the same or drop, even where substantial wage increases occur. At the same time, as we saw with the labor paradox, wage increases guarantee that the cost of care services in the transductive sector will rise more than proportionately, with the result that eventually these and related activities will price themselves out of the market. As a result, the economic order we now have, whose nucleus is still market-driven production growth, has a built-in tendency to increase its degree of industrialization, even to the point where industrial substitutes increasingly replace our experience of nature and the outdoors (as the rising popularity of amusement parks, for example, indicates).

The industrial paradox is a complete anomaly in our modern-day society. For increased industrialization, which rising prosperity brings, accelerates pressure on the environment and on energy precisely as it obstructs our ability to care for people and the environment! It therefore shows us that our current economic order poses a perilous danger to sustainability. It is the first signal that our economic order is fraught with shortcomings and is internally out of date.

1. Dutch economist S. D. Eikelboom named this paradox in a dissertation at Erasmus University entitled *De Industriële Paradox* (1987).

General Scarcity

Closely related to this is a second remarkable phenomenon, alluded to in Chapter 1. In his book *The Realm of Scarcity,* social philosopher Hans Achterhuis points out that in previous centuries the word "scarcity" was never used in a general sense.[2] Of course, there were critical shortages of certain goods from time to time, but in previous centuries people possessed no notion of scarcity *in general,* as we do today. Generalized scarcity, perhaps best seen in the enormous and increasingly permanent government deficits in the West, is a thoroughly modern phenomenon, and it afflicts only industrialized economies.

How on earth did general scarcity arise? Again, how is it possible that a society of unprecedented wealth also experiences unprecedented scarcity? Here we meet the scarcity paradox mentioned in Chapter 1: one would expect that as prosperity grew and incomes rose, society would have met more needs, and that as a result general scarcity would have *declined* rather than risen. This paradox shouts out at us every day from the pages of newspapers and from news reports. Even as economic growth continues and the average level of material prosperity rises, we read reports indicating that businesses, nonprofit organizations, and governments have had to slash essential expenditures — reports that appear much more frequently today than they did twenty-five years ago, when the average income was half of what it is today.

Here, too, the explanation for the anomaly is simple, but the consequences are immense. General scarcity has arisen because, despite the explosion of our economic means, our needs have burgeoned much faster than the means for meeting them.

Like the industrial paradox, this startling increase of economic need *precisely* at a time of unprecedented material prosperity is thoroughly baffling. As we saw in Chapter 2, current economic thinking suggests that we must alleviate society's critical care needs by vigorously increasing production and by deploying continually better applications of scarce production factors. In order to do this, contemporary economics very conveniently accepts all human needs as given, as neutral. Economic science today therefore works hand in glove with our

2. Hans Achterhuis, *Het Rijk van de Schaarste: van Thomas Hobbes tot Michel Foucault* [The Realm of Scarcity: from Thomas Hobbes to Michel Foucault] (Baarn: Ambo, 1988).

economic order, which brings together more and more means so that individuals and communities can meet these needs as well as possible. But what if, through the operation of our economic processes, the needs of people increase faster than this assembling of resources? Then honesty requires us to admit that really from that point forward many things have happened for nothing; the end result has been that our experience of scarcity in the West has increased more than our experience of prosperity. Incessantly putting every emphasis on expanding production further is then like laying down a carpet that gets rolled up from behind more quickly then it gets installed in front.

Today, needs in our society have become floating and weightless, as if possessing no gravity. We no longer anchor them in what we truly need; instead, we allow an economic process that *requires* needs in order to continue functioning to give them their definition.

General scarcity, then, is the second strong signal that our economic system is fundamentally out of date. It is no longer able to stand up to the demands of our time. It has set out on a path toward what the German philosopher Hegel more than a century and a half ago called "false infinity," by which he meant to describe the limitless explosion of needs in bourgeois society.[3]

Yet an enigma remains. How is it that the needs of people have increased faster than their incomes? It is true that advertising is a powerful weapon. But does the power of advertising alone adequately explain these soaring needs? Have deeper-lying factors also played a role? Indeed they have.

Consider the role that our experience of *time* plays in the escalation of need in today's materially prosperous society. Goods and services require time to buy and to use. They also take time to maintain, repair, and eventually replace. Television, for example, consumes an inordinate amount of time. *Things* take up more and more time in a materially prosperous society, and less time remains for interaction with people. As S. B. Linder has shown, people in a materially rich culture have the tendency to be more harried as well as more lonely or isolated.[4] This is not all, however: lack of time has created new

3. Georg Wilhelm Friedrich Hegel, *The Philosophy of Right,* trans. with notes by T. M. Knox (Chicago: Encyclopedia Britannica, 1955).
4. S. B. Linder, *The Harried Leisure Class* (New York: Columbia University, 1970).

markets and production streams whose sole purpose is to save us time. The main selling point of a number of household appliances is that they save time, which is then supposed to leave us more time for other work or for raising children, for example. But does not the fact that all of our life is finite suggest that a ceiling limits what we can meaningfully possess? While we can attempt to alter this ceiling by producing and consuming more and more time-saving goods, ironically this alteration consumes additional time. In a similar vein, a reputable computer analyst has recently argued that our interaction with computer technologies has produced a net *loss* of time, a loss that he suggests largely explains the outcome of a recent Harvard study showing that whatever discernible impact information technologies have had on productivity has been negative, not positive.[5]

But let us go a level deeper. In a number of writings the renowned French philosopher René Girard has suggested that "desire" in Western society has peculiar traits. The peculiarity is not that one person desires things because the other already has them or also wants them. Girard argues that this type of desire, which he calls "mimetic" or "triangular," has been a trademark of human society since the beginning of the world. But the peculiarity of our Western society lies in the *cure* we have chosen for remedying the continual escalation of material desires, desires that intensify as people become more like each other and then imitate each other more and more. Our Western remedy has been to continually increase the production of products. The reasoning goes like this: if we make more products available on a mass scale, then what one person desires and possesses the other person who desires can *also* possess. From this vantage point, two adherents of Girard's approach note that our society has clearly rooted its inner cultural stability in the quasi-certainty that economic growth will continue forever.[6] This further suggests that as soon as economic growth stops, the whole enterprise could easily collapse, as unsatiated desire leads to social unrest, violence, and revolution.

The picture that René Girard paints is not encouraging; its colors

5. Stephen Levy, "The Case of Purloined Productivity," *MacWorld,* March 1993, 57-60. The irony is not lost on the author that industry introduced information technologies largely to save time and increase productivity.

6. Paul Dumouchel and Jean Pierre Dupey, *L'enfer des Choses: René Girard et la Logique de le'economie* (Paris: Seuil, 1979).

are laid on thickly and darkly. Yet he has made it disconcertingly clear that an economic growth whose primary motivation is material desire knows of no end. For if we permit our material desire no other measure than that which the other possesses, then the end will never come. This, too, then is a signal that "needs" in our society are now "floating"; we anchor them less and less in the reality of what people actually need to live, or in genuine economic needs.

The Human Condition

In our judgment, Hannah Arendt offers perhaps the most profound analysis of what is happening in Western culture and its economic order. Her analysis provides the third and most critical signal that our contemporary economic order is out of touch with reality and therefore out of date. She wrote her book *The Human Condition* during the era of the first trips into outer space, trips in which she detects something of a desire by modern humanity to escape from the earth. Modern humanity, Arendt argues, considers the earth fraught with too many limitations.

By "the human condition" Arendt means those conditions that are essential for people to live as real people. She identifies three such conditions. The first is *social life* in its plurality: we cannot be human without the other. In fact, we are born from a community of two. The second condition is a relationship with the *earth* ("earthlyness"); we are bound to nature, whether we like it or not, in both its living and its dead forms. Finally, the human condition contains a relationship with *time* ("life itself"). Time not only places us between generations but carries us forward from birth through childhood, adulthood, and death.

What, meanwhile, has become the trademark of Western society? Obviously, argues Hannah Arendt, we have increasingly viewed the three basic conditions of our being human not as that which forms the substance of life but as restrictions — restrictions that interfere with our desires. For do we not consider it disgraceful to be dependent on others? And do we not find it irritating when nature begins to place limits on our desires? And do not many of us experience aging as a curse? In this manner we transform the three conditions that make life and culture possible into obstacles and hindrances instead.

There is more, however. For in our time our culture has learned to put faith in progress. This has created the possibility of construing these obstacles and hindrances as barriers that we can overcome using every available technological and economic means. The directive then becomes this: let us manufacture as many consumption products as possible, so that no one needs to be dependent on others; let us manufacture substitute raw materials if the original raw materials threaten to give out; and let us apply all of our medical knowledge and resources to extending life wherever possible!

The importance of Hannah Arendt's analysis is not just that it provides us with a key to better understand why our society's demand for products, substitute raw materials, and health care have burgeoned. More significantly, her analysis demonstrates that we must see the explosion of means required to satisfy our escalating material desires as a sign of a titanic battle against the human condition itself. Indeed, what is happening now with current processes of endless economic growth is not *real* anymore. It has no root in the human condition itself. It no longer helps people to live in peace with their destiny. Donning the mask of realism, our economic order has mounted the most idealist live performance that this world has ever seen, a performance that casts heavy shadows not only over our environment and the increasingly impoverished Third World but also over Western humanity *itself.* For in today's context, the more affluent we become, the more we alienate ourselves from our *own* created human condition.

We may then draw yet another conclusion. Evidently the critical problems in today's world form mirror images. Just as racism seems to be a black problem but in reality is a white problem, so too the problem of poverty is rooted first and foremost in our inability to deal with wealth. Similarly, the problem of the degenerating environment mirrors the still deeper problem that we do not wish to accept *ourselves* in our earthly and creaturely condition.

Our economic order has had, and still has, many good sides. Some, such as the respect for human freedom, ought to be maintained. But we must state that our economic order sets our society out on the wrong foot. It draws us away from our human condition and from what we genuinely need to sustain culture and aims us at what is not real instead. It breaks apart culture and the world into the fragments of its own ambitions. Consequently, our economic order is thoroughly out of date and must, with utmost urgency, be replaced.

A Doorway of Hope

We may now draw the themes of these last two chapters together. For now we can clearly make out more than a crack in the wall: we can see a widening expanse opening up onto a possibly brighter future.

People can hold on to illusions for a long time, they can cut loose the rudder steering their economic needs, and they can surrender to the hypnosis of always needing to accumulate more. But in the long run they do this at the expense of their own humanity. This then brings them to a fundamental choice. Hannah Arendt argues here that in such choices people are also bound to their inalienable human condition. They cannot simply continue to deny their human condition, for if they did so they would isolate themselves from their neighbors, from the earth, and from time. In other words, they would do so at the expense of their humanity and of all that they treasure. We may therefore expect — indeed, we already see it happening — that public concern for the future and popular movements will focus on precisely those areas where the ongoing progress of our growth-driven society threatens our human condition itself. Popular movements often derive their greatest strength from what people are no longer willing to accept. The strength of the peace movement during the Cold War did not lie in well-formulated proposals but in the fact that people realized deep down that the arms race could not continue. So also today: where human society persistently deteriorates in a number of areas, where we ceaselessly pollute the environment, and where we "hurry" time along, there potential areas of transformation and renewal will surface. People will make it known that things may no longer continue as they are and as they have been. They will no longer take it.

But if we believe that popular movements automatically advance the common good, then we do not know the lessons of history. It will therefore be crucial to point to certain initiatives that have prepared the way, to concrete examples that demonstrate that things can be different. Then, as a positive expression of its protest, our society can dig channels toward an economy of care.

Let us harbor no illusions that the road to renewal will be easy. Consider again the current exercise of economic power. What does implementing caring administration mean in terms of the exercise of economic control? In line with the position taken by the ecumenical movement since its inception, we believe that it implies moving toward shared or "differentiated responsibility" in society, or toward a so-called responsible society in which all sectors of society assume responsibility for their economic actions. In a responsible society the production sector, for example, must internalize rather than externalize its effects. In other words, one can no longer assume that other sectors, such as the government, will attempt to redress one's own harmful effects.

It is precisely here that we encounter perhaps our most formidable barrier. A society in which people have grown accustomed to accepting the authority of what we might call a "double self-evidence" — the self-evidence that we must materially progress, and the self-evidence that we have every right to expel the environmental and social effects of this progress to other people or sectors — will not easily permit its transformation into a genuinely responsible society. We may even describe the force of this resistance in religious language. Today both Christians and non-Christians interact with the forces of scientific, technological, and economic progress in the same manner that people interact with idols. Just as historically ancient ideologies or religions, caught up in the pursuit of prosperity and security, summoned forth their own gods (represented by images of the forces of nature, for example), so too today, caught up in the pursuit of prosperity and security, our ideology of material prosperity has evoked its own gods (the forces of modernization: economic growth, technological development, scientific advancement, and the unrestricted expansion of the market or the state). But our gods have betrayed us. They require sacrifices in exchange for providing us with material prosperity — mounting poverty, the destruction of health and the environment, the relentless elimination of jobs and the quality of work, and the perpetual return of the threat of war. Yet time after time we are told in tones borne up by the weight of "self-evidence" that these sacrifices are necessary, if not "preordained."[7]

The cultural renewal required today therefore has the depth and breadth of a conversion. It means pointing our lives in the opposite direction, away from more and more for ourselves and the concentration of power that accompanies this to enough and the shared or differentiated responsibility that supports it. We will not accomplish this simply by knocking technological progress and economic growth off of their pedestals. Rather, we must make both of these serviceable

---

7. For a more extensive discussion of this theme, see Bob Goudzwaard, *Idols of Our Time,* trans. Mark R. Vander Vennen (Downers Grove, Ill.: InterVarsity Press, 1984).

to the requirements of a responsible society. They must serve the poor, the health of people and the environment, and dignity in the work-place. If we do not accept such a conversion, then the risk increases that we will replace our current gods with gods even more tyrannical. Our culture therefore faces the dilemma of *choosing* which god it will serve and which accompanying life-style it will follow, the same dilemma that confronted the people of God in the Scriptures (see, for example, Deuteronomy 30; 1 Kings 18; Luke 12).

Concrete Initiatives

At first glance, the approach we outlined in Chapter 4 may have seemed utopian. But already in this chapter we have attempted to show that our appeal is in fact realistic. Realism, however, implies that the approach must be workable in practice. And can we claim that this approach is realistic in this sense?

Perhaps two remarks will help. First, the comments offered above demonstrate that we do not advocate a sudden revolutionist change of our entire economic order. Rather, we must suggest how a natural but fundamental change can occur from within our existing economic order. We have attempted to show that this change has already begun spontaneously in a number of areas in our society.

We therefore advocate a "dual" economy as an interim phase, an economy in which the old and new coexist. During this phase society can acquaint itself with steps toward a renewed economic order and with the possibility of implementing an alternative approach to economic ends, means, and power. An important initiative in acquainting ourselves with a renewed economic order would be to invite to the decision-making table those responsible movements or bodies that bring with them considerations other than those of unrestricted economic expansion, considerations that relate to the human condition. For example, those movements or bodies now active in specific fields of care, such as sustainable agriculture and environmental organizations, antipoverty bodies and health organizations, ought to be involved in the making of our society's most important socioeconomic decisions, including those of wage and salary development. This initiative could in itself gradually increase the readiness within our society to move toward restricting consumption and income levels.

Secondly, what we appeal for here has not fallen out of the blue sky. Important examples already exist. Whether on a small or a large scale, some people in various industries and trade unions have consciously chosen to limit their own material desires and the incomes that support these in order to use them as instruments for creating employment aimed at meeting unmet needs. In Sweden, for example, 1 percent of annual income has been designated to improving working conditions in the workplace. Along with the Dutch MEMO companies, in the Netherlands the Dutch Christian Labor Union (CNV) has recently offered to freeze wage increase demands for a five-year period in exchange for more care devoted to the environment and to the poor as well as a negotiated increase in the number of jobs available. The largest industrial labor union in western Germany, I-G Metall, has offered to freeze real wages for five years in exchange for more jobs, especially in the eastern part of Germany. Residents of most of the provinces of Canada can invest moneys in "worker investment" funds. Operated under the auspices of labor federations and matched by 20 percent tax deductions from both the federal and provincial governments, these funds are invested in small to medium-sized companies that are relatively labor-intensive. It is generally acknowledged that Quebec's Solidarity Fund, for example, has helped to maintain employment levels in that province.

In western Kenya, under a contractual agreement with a British-based multinational sugar company, thirty-four thousand families farm their own land, only 60 percent of which can be used for export production. The remainder must be used for local subsistence. This arrangement has led to a stoppage in Kenyan imports of sugar; to labor-intensive, low-yield farming that produces surpluses without exhausting the soil; and to local ownership of the large sugarcane mill. Meanwhile, profits from the mill are reinvested in the community and have helped to develop an excellent school system and a network of modern health clinics. Similarly, the Basque region of Spain boasts a vital forty-year tradition of locally operated and owned cooperatives, a tradition that largely accounts for the economic, social, and environmental viability of the region.

Moreover, in North America forms of sustainable agriculture and cooperative, local-community economic development are springing up. In 1990 the small northern Ontario town of Kapuskasing banded together and raised $15 million to rescue and purchase the local pulp and paper mill, a mill that was the mainstay of the community. Though some costs have been high, there have been many benefits: management and labor had to set aside their mistrust, five unions had to abandon old antagonisms to become part owners (each employee is a shareholder), the plant is being upgraded to meet environmental standards, and the mill was one of few pulp and paper mills in North America to make a profit in 1992.

In the United States comparable local community development efforts are under way in both urban and rural settings. The land trust movement, in which land is purchased and held in perpetuity, especially for the purpose of creating affordable housing, has attracted considerable attention. Sustainable agricultural practices are on the increase, and applications of alternative forms of energy are becoming more and more mainstream.[8] Similarly, in the care sector of the economy, the rapid emergence in many states of "wraparound," or individualized, services for children and adolescents is striking. With individualized services, youth who are severely emotionally and behaviorally challenged remain in their own homes or communities instead of being sent to out-of-state residential treatment. To make this happen, children's service agencies break down traditional interagency barriers, jointly embrace the concept of "unconditional care" (that is, they agree never to give up on the child and family and never to eject them from the service), and reallocate their own existing resources to create a flexible pool of dollars that can be used for whatever is required to keep the child in the community. Collaborating agencies then alter the structure of control, so that parents become full participants in all of the decisions made about their child (including how to use the funds), while at the same time drawing in persons from the family's surroundings who know the child and family best — such as a neighbor, a relative, an older friend — and paying them appropriately to provide essential services. In other words, individualized services draw in the informal transductive sector, legitimize it, and link it to the professional sector in groundbreaking ways. Significantly, though researchers express caution, comparison studies show that not only are wraparound services generally more cost-effective

---

8. The June 1993 issue of the Washington Times's *The World and I* states that the energy presently generated by wind turbines in California can power all of the residences of San Francisco (Darrell Dodge, "Wind Power Rising," *The World and I* 8, no. 6 [June 1993]: 190).

than institutional residential treatment but also the outcomes for children and youth are markedly better.[9]

In all of this, elements of a new economic order have sprung up spontaneously in the midst of our existing economy.[10]

Here, too, we refer to the ruminations carried on for several years in the ecumenical community about a "sustainable economy," ruminations to which economists such as Herman Daly have contributed.[11] But we also refer to concrete scenarios that have already been worked out. For example, in 1983 the Netherlands Scientific Council for Government Policy, a research arm of the Dutch government, published a study entitled *A Policy-Oriented Survey of the Future.*[12] The council attempted to trace the future of the Netherlands over a ten-year period (commencing with the date of the report) assuming the country's adoption of one of

9. Individualized services are witnessing a virtual explosion of activity. Sites are in operation in over thirty states, while several states, including Vermont, Virginia, Alaska, Oregon, and others, have legislatively mandated individualized services, in some instances creating the flexible funds required from out of the dollars that would have sent the child to residential treatment. For an overview of individualized services, see L. Adlai Boyd, "Integrating Systems of Care for Children and Families: An Overview of Values, Methods and Characteristics of Developing Models, with Examples and Recommendations" (Tampa, Fla: Department of Child and Family Studies, Florida Mental Health Institute, University of South Florida, July 1992); Judith W. Katz-Leavy, Ira S. Lourie, Beth A. Stroul, Chris Zeigler-Dendy, "Individualized Services in a System of Care" (Washington, D.C.: CASSP Technical Assistance Centre, Center for Child Health & Mental Health Policy, Georgetown University Child Development Center, July 1992); and John D. Burchard, Sara D. Burchard, Robert Sewell, John VanDenBerg, "One Kid at a Time: A Case Study Evaluation of the Alaska Youth Initiative Demonstration Project" (Washington, D.C.: CASSP Technical Assistance Centre, Center for Child Health & Mental Health Policy, Georgetown University Child Development Center, June 1993). In terms of the structure of control, in many instances parents act as their own case managers.

10. Some of the examples described here are taken from a television special produced by the Canadian Broadcasting Corporation (CDC) entitled "Trading Futures. Living in the Global Economy," a Special Report with David Suzuki, which aired on CBC television on April 4, 1993.

11. See, for example, Daly's *Steady State Economics* (Washington, D.C.: Island Press, 1991).

12. Netherlands Scientific Council for Government Policy, *Beleidsgerichte Toekomstverkenningen: Deel 2: Een Verruiming van Perspectief* [A Policy-Oriented Survey of the Future: Towards a Broader Perspective] (The Hague: Staatsuitgeverij, 1983). An extensive English summary is available. The address of the council is Plein 1813, nr. 2, 2514 JN, The Hague, The Netherlands.

three scenarios: (1) a further expansion of the market economy; (2) an extension of the welfare state; or (3) the implementation of the economics of enough (alternately called in the report "a sustainable society," "the economics of care," and "the economics of voluntary austerity"). With the help of a Leontieff-type input/output model, to which, because of the requirements of the "sustainable society" perspective, a "quality of work" category was added, a research group of the council projected the likely outcomes of each of the three scenarios. In its groundbreaking accompanying research study entitled *The Limits and Possibilities of the Economic System in Holland,* the research group concluded that the economics of enough would have a more favorable impact than either the market economy or welfare state scenarios on employment levels, the quality of work, the environment, energy savings, capital transfer to the Third World, and government deficits, if the Dutch people were willing simply to *maintain* average income and consumption levels at their present plane (in no year was there a decrease in income and consumption of more than 3 percent), and if they were willing to cooperate in orienting society, as a whole and in its parts, to these broader ends.[13]

The latter study also explores in detail what each of the three scenarios (also called "export-led growth," "consumption-oriented growth," and "stewardship") would achieve in terms of specific policy objectives. With respect to minimizing unemployment, the researchers found that the economics of enough would decrease unemployment *substantially* more than *either* of the other two scenarios (by approximately twice as much), if the Dutch people were willing to accept, in exchange for a higher quantity and quality of work, a maximum reduction of 5 percent in their level of consumption. The study notes that "thanks to the relatively painless goal restrictions, very favorable values are found for the goal variables, with exceptional optimization."[14]

Naturally, these calculations have limitations, which both studies acknowledge. But on the basis of these and other studies, we may state definitively that the "economics of enough" is not a phantom. Rather, it is a *viable* scenario. It possesses an intrinsic, internally rigorous consistency.

13. Netherlands Scientific Council for Government Policy, *De Grenzen en Mogelijkheden van het Economisch Stelsel in Nederland* [The Limits and Possibilities of the Economic System in Holland] (The Hague: Staatsuitgeverij, 1983).
14. Ibid., 105.

CHAPTER 6

Sustainable Development

In 1987 the World Commission on Environment and Development published the report *Our Common Future*. Established by the United Nations, this commission, chaired by Norwegian Prime Minister Brundtland, was broadly constituted. Its task was to define the relationship between development and the environment. The problem posed for the commission was this: how can we achieve an economic development that provides for the needs of today's generation without endangering future generations? Thanks largely to the Brundtland report, the environment returned to the political agenda, from which it had virtually disappeared, especially because of the actions of the Reagan administration. This process reached a culmination at the Earth Summit (UNCED) held in Rio de Janeiro, Brazil, in 1992, ably chaired by Maurice Strong.

Maurice Strong, who presently serves as the chairman and chief executive officer of Ontario Hydro, was eminently suited to the daunting task of secretary general of UNCED. A well-known Canadian entrepreneur and corporate executive (as well as the Canadian representative on the Brundtland Commission), Strong has been a longstanding proponent of economic renewal. In 1978 he declared:

> Our commitment to continuous growth in gross national product is built right into the economic system by which modern industrialized societies function. It is based on the assumption that more is better, that the well-being of the societies can only be assured by continuous growth in the material sense. . . . [But] in industrialized

112

societies *most of the valid needs as yet unsatisfied are of a non-material nature. But industry rarely searches these out as they do not accord with traditional industrial logic.*[1]

Strong adds:

> The response of our industrial machine is to expand its markets by creating new wants and new appetites amongst the people who can afford them. We are thus caught in a paradox in which we have created an industrial system capable of meeting the basic needs of all the world's people but are in fact using it largely to foster further growth in the demand by the wealthy minority for goods and services well beyond what we need or is good for us.[2]

Finally, he states:

> Our attitudes towards growth are at the heart of the present dilemma of industrial civilization. This is the disease which has spread through the body of modern technological societies. This "growth disease" has within it the potential for self-destruction of our society. . . . The challenge we now face is nothing less than that of creating a whole new approach to the growth of our society, to the goals of growth, to the processes of growth, and to the systems of incentives and penalties which determine our patterns of growth.[3]

As part of the sustainable-development debate, a worldwide discussion has begun about how we ought to measure economic development. Along with Al Gore, Herman Daly, Bernard Cobb, and many others, we hold the conviction that the current measure, the gross national product (GNP) (a measure that is used even by the United Nations) is antiquated.[4] The GNP registers only transactions that have

1. Quoted in Gerald Vandezande, *Christians in the Crisis* (Toronto: Anglican Book Centre, 1984), 47; Strong's italics.
2. Ibid.
3. Ibid.
4. In *Earth in the Balance* (New York: Houghton Mifflin Company, 1992), Al Gore calls for changing "the definition of the GNP . . . to include environmental costs and benefits" (346). And he minces no words: "There is no excuse for not changing the definition of the GNP" (338).

a monetary value. Sustainable development, however, requires an entirely different measure, because certain critical realities do not enter the measure, such as the realities that current production methods use up stocks of raw materials, energy, and the environment, and that in many places they leave behind severe pollution that will require future generations to lay out enormous amounts of money. It was therefore for good reason that the participants at the Earth Summit discussed the issue of bringing current production methods and consumption patterns in line with what we understand as sustainability.

Let us note also that the issue of sustainable development is poignant for the nations of the Third World. When one consults the report *The Challenge to the South,* published in 1990, it is difficult to suppress a sense of disappointment.[5] Page after page of the report describes significant ecological deterioration. The report correctly points out that "the North is responsible for the bulk of the damage to the environment because of its waste life-style."[6] Equally forceful in presenting its own model of development, the report draws the conclusion that "the South has no alternative but to pursue a path of rapid economic growth, and hence to industrialize; it must therefore take action to control the environmental hazards to accompany such growth."[7]

When the issue is addressing the changes required in international political and economic policy, many Third World countries hesitate to give the environmental debate equal status with the need to alleviate poverty. They fear that the North will use the need to preserve the environment as an argument against the industrialization of the South (though we find an encouraging example of a breakthrough in the emergence of the Consumers Association of Penang [CAP] in Malasia, in response to Japanese lumber companies' destruction of tropical virgin forests).

The Brundtland report made very clear that poverty itself puts heavy pressure on the environment. This confronts us with a fundamental dilemma that seems to call for the formulation of an alternative, non-Western model of development. Such a model would emphasize meeting basic subsistence needs, but in reference to the

---

5. Independent Commission of the South on Development Issues, *The Challenge to the South* (Oxford: Oxford University Press, 1990).

6. Ibid.

7. Ibid.

categorization developed in Chapter 4, it would also seek to provide items lying immediately above the absolute minimum required, such as bicycles and second sets of clothing. But one can expect that the production of these goods in the Third World, goods meeting the subsistence and related needs of up to one billion people, will put extreme pressure on the environment, especially because of the increased use of fertilizers. We therefore draw the inescapable conclusion that the industrialized countries must establish a ceiling on their own production and consumption, combined with an adequate level for production and consumption in the South.

Back in 1974, the second report of the Club of Rome raised this issue. In *Mankind at the Turning Point,* authors Mesarovic and Pestel posed this question: "Isn't it legitimate to ask, as representatives of the developing countries, whether there should be maximum limits on consumption . . . ?"[8]

In what may be instructive for other industrialized regions, the Dutch National Advisory Council for Development Cooperation formulated this need in a presentation to the European Community. Its brief stated:

> If the developing countries find themselves compelled to implement a different model of development on ecological grounds, then the need for sustainable development becomes that much more acute for countries within the European Community itself. Per capita, the industrial countries exercise much higher demand on the world's scarce and exhaustible resources than do the developing countries. We will seriously damage the credibility of the European Community's positive assessment of the Brundtland report if the Community itself is not prepared to change its own policy. We cannot expect the poor countries to strive for sustainable development if the member states of the European Community do not lead the way.

The Brundtland report touted the conviction that we must pursue continuous economic growth in order to eliminate current economic differentials. Regrettably, it left unanswered the question of whether such growth can coincide with the slackening of pressure

8. Mihajlo Mesarovic and Eduard Pestel, *Mankind at the Turning Point* (New York: Dutton, 1974), 69.

115

on the environment that is required for sustainability. But in what we consider a major advance, the UNCED conference corrected this flaw. The pressure of events helped to bring about this achievement. Specifically, as we saw in Chapter 1, in spite of great efforts by many, in spite of the availability of modern technology and a greatly expanded knowledge of organizational issues, the total number of poor people in the world has risen. Similarly, the 1992 *Human Development Report* reports that "between 1960 and 1989, the countries with the richest 20% of the world's population increased their share of the global Gross National Product from 70.2% to 82.7% . . . while the countries with the poorest 20% of the world population saw their share fall from 2.3% to 1.4%."[9] This development counteracts the legitimate desire to direct world production toward meeting the basic subsistence needs of more than one billion poor people in Asia, Africa, and Latin America. Further, if priority were given to production for meeting these basic subsistence needs, this would signify an even greater infringement upon the environmental space available, as such production would also impinge upon the environment. In this light, it is no wonder that at UNCED the representatives of the developing countries stressed heavily the environmental responsibility of the rich nations, as they are the largest polluters. About 75 percent of all environmental damage is caused by the 25 percent of the world's population who live in the North. It was thus self-evident — at least to the developing countries at UNCED — that it is precisely this group of people who, by means of their production and consumption patterns, exhaust the carrying capacity of the environment.

Against the backdrop of these dilemmas, a heated exchange took place in Brazil between representatives of the developing countries and those of the industrialized countries. In order to gain cooperation from the developing countries to help solve environmental problems, the industrialized countries promised to review the applied production methods and the usual consumption patterns in their own countries, with a view to changing them. We read this in Chapter 4 of Agenda 21.[10]

9. As cited in the World Council of Churches, *Christian Faith and the World Economy Today* (Geneva: WCC Publications, 1992), 18.

10. Nicholas A. Robinson, ed., *Agenda 21 and the UNCED Proceedings* (New York: Oceana Publications Ltd., 1992).

With these concrete promises, the industrialized nations now stand on the threshold of a sweeping process of change, *if* of course they can summon the readiness and political will to do so.

Meanwhile, by linking the word "sustainable" with the word "development," the Brundtland Commission assured that the concept of development will no longer be tied solely to events unfolding in the countries of the South. Sustainable development is now a concept that has far-reaching consequences for the so-called developed countries. For the linkage of sustainability with development implies that perhaps something has gone wrong in the development of the *developed* countries.

When it comes to production methods in the North, we observe that, compared to a number of years ago, business, especially industry, now pays more attention to using raw materials and energy more scrupulously and to reusing materials. In agriculture, however, exhaustion of resources and pollution proceed relatively unabated.

Much discussion has also taken place about whether alterations in the price system can protect and preserve the environment. One proposal put forward in the European Community is to institute a "carbon energy tax." Industry officials have vigorously opposed such proposals, because they fear that if only the member states of the European Community pay this tax, then the competitive position of industry in Europe will suffer in comparison to the United States and Japan. The counterargument made by environmentalists is that it is shortsighted simply to wait for others to act. The environmental movement in the Netherlands holds the position, which we support, that the European Community ought to raise energy prices, lower other taxes for industry, and invite the United States, Canada, and Japan to do the same. If they reject the invitation, then the Community could reply by raising tariffs on energy-intensive products. In this connection, we also ought to introduce a higher sales tax on materially and environmentally intensive products, and a lower sales tax on environmentally friendly and labor-intensive products (including services from repair-oriented companies).

When it comes to consumption patterns today, we observe that more and more people are prepared to alter their own behavior when it comes to the environment. Nevertheless, because of steady increases in total available income, which still forms the goal of virtually every government, less overall pressure on the environment is out of the question, while a discernible drop in the total number of poor people throughout the world is even less thinkable.

The UNCED conference also facilitated broad consultations among nongovernment organizations (NGOs) active in the field of development and the environment. These NGOs drafted a laudable *Treaty on Consumption and Lifestyle,* part of which we shall cite:

> Overall consumption and production must be eased back to fit within the regenerative carrying capacity of the earth. Given the ecological and development crisis, this transition must be completed within a few decades in order to avoid irreversible damage to life on earth.

> The use of energy, especially fossil fuels, must be reduced significantly. Renewable sources which are less environmentally damaging should be promoted.

> Due to their destructive social and environmental impacts, production and use of military goods and weapons are not an acceptable part of an equitable and environmentally sustainable society.

> Production and consumption of products with built-in obsolescence should be stopped; consumption of products which are transported over long distances should be reduced; and production processes which create toxic, hazardous or radioactive wastes should be halted.

> Reduction in consumption should have priority over reuse or recycling of products.

Finally, we hear a unique echo of the theme begun by the Brundtland report in the worldwide conciliary process that the World Council of Churches began at its Vancouver Assembly in 1989. The themes of "Justice, Peace and the Integrity of Creation" dovetail with the issues raised in this book. The "Closing Declaration" of the European Ecumenical Conference on Peace and Justice held in Basel, Switzerland, in 1989 witnessed to the need to meet primary subsistence needs as quickly as possible. It also stated that a national defense can no longer offer protection and security, and it contained a convincing appeal to establish an international ecological order. After the UNCED conference, the World Council of Churches declared: "One important contribution that the churches can make to the UNCED process is to speak clearly to the indivisible connections between these issues, and of the impossibility of addressing them in isolation from one another. . . . We want to say as forcefully as we can that social justice for all people and eco-justice for all creation must go together." Shortly thereafter the World Council of Churches affirmed this statement by publishing a study document entitled *Christian Faith and the World Economy Today*.[11]

Conclusion

The implementation of Agenda 21, or an agenda for the twenty-first century, does not need to wait for the end of this century. In fact, it is in the twentieth century that the battle to banish the causes of poverty and environmental degradation has begun. The political art will be to address both issues together, rather than one at the expense of the other. The new agenda requires reconstructing society, both nationally and internationally. Sustainability and justice are at stake. It is high time that the current agenda of economics, both in theory and in practice, becomes attuned to the broader agenda that was provisionally drawn up in Rio de Janeiro.

11. Cited above in n. 9.

CHAPTER 7

Answering the Objections

In this chapter we shall address a number of objections frequently voiced against renewing the economy.

Objection 1: What about "Human Nature"?

It is self-evident that what undergirds today's economic system and economic theory is our pursuit of the "acquisitive society." This pursuit both drives our economic process and results from that process. Our desire for more material products plays a central role in our society, so central that we frequently hear it described today as a basic trait of human nature. When discussing the patterns of today's economic practice in the light of the prospects for economic renewal, we often hear the phrase "but that's how people are," or "that's human nature," or "people are greedy by nature." We forget, of course, that people are also *formed* one way or another.

Let us then review those traits of "human nature" that people use to defend today's economic order or to reject the possibility of renewing it. There are several.

Perhaps the most common argument, alluded to above, is that because people are greedy by nature, economic renewal is out of the question.

A second anthropologically based defense of the present economic order is that increased possessions serve to compensate for the dwindling satisfaction of work. Economists such as Irving Fetscher

120

have linked mounting alienation in the workplace with the drive to consume: consumption, Fetscher argues, fills a vacuum created at work. He writes: "Just as the body, which no longer experiences the exertion of physical work, has the compensation of sport, so too the unfulfilled soul has the compensation of luxury." This then serves as a rationale for continuing our current economic patterns.

A third defense of our present economic order and its operation is that people need to acquire a sufficient amount of wealth in order to safeguard themselves against potential insecurity and vulnerability in the future. Western society has structured itself in such a way that difficult circumstances throw us back upon ourselves. If, through accident or disease, one can no longer participate in the economic process, then the government's safety net provides a minimal benefit. But this is virtually all that is available: by and large we can no longer really appeal to our immediate neighbor and/or to the broader community, such as our neighborhood or town. The forces of individualism in our society have all but eliminated this possibility. As a consequence, those who find themselves in difficult circumstances must "earn" whatever they require over and above that which a minimal government benefit provides, regardless of whether this is in the realm of possibility. Our employment today must therefore supply not only what we require to meet our needs and material desires today but also a nest egg as a margin against the uncertainties of the future. This, too, serves to bolster the continuation of our pursuit of economic growth.

A fourth defense of our present economic order rests on assumptions about human motivation. Today we hear the argument that lopsided income distribution, together with the dissimilar consumption opportunities it brings, motivates people to intensify their own involvement in the production process. This argument amounts to a social explanation for why we have increased our efforts, individually and collectively, to expand production. It replaces the metaphysical explanation of poverty that gradually fell out of favor after the end of the eighteenth century. Gradually society transformed poverty into an economic and political problem requiring a solution. Paradoxically, however, at the same time many people also argued that poverty provided the best motivation for work. They viewed hunger, for instance, as an effective means for stimulating industriousness. The modern variation of this paradox, namely, that we must maintain "sufficiently large" income differentials in order to keep motivation and industriousness alive, amounts to a defense for continuing and expanding the acquisitive society.

People thus appeal to at least four traits of human nature to help defend the present economic order and its priorities: greed; the human need to compensate for the loss of job satisfaction; the need to build up a nest egg in the face of possible hardship in the future; and the human need to have the fear of poverty serve as a motivation for work. Ironically, a renewed economy would remove the conditions that cause several of these traits to flourish.

But what we wish to dispute here is the assumption that these human behaviors and reactions apply at all times and in all respects. In other words, we reject the one-sided premise that these traits are anthropologically *constant*. Those who argue that they are constant reject in principle any appeal for change or reversal. And it is their rejection, in our view, that creates the sluggishness by which the process of economic renewal moves today. Of course, we must have realistic expectations about change and its pace. But it is our conviction that the current lack of change is due to *neglect*, not to *inability*. Neglect has to do with ignoring things, with refusing to see things as they are.

It strikes us, in contrast, that people behave both as a genuine neighbor and as an enemy. While no single societal order can cancel out or neutralize this ambivalence, every societal order *orients* its members in one or the other direction. No societal order is indifferent or neutral. Our present social and economic order encourages people to pursue individual self-interest at the expense of community, neighborliness, and freedom for all. Further, both capitalism and socialism set out first to exploit the dissimilarities in people's capabilities and endowments, and then to temper somewhat the excesses.

But a renewed societal and economic order would seek to encourage and reward community and freedom for all. As already described, we envision a society whose primary concern at the national and international levels is to encourage the right to life of the other, both now and in the future; a society, in other words, in which the alleviation of suffering, injustice, violence, and oppression is paramount. To help bring this about, we seek to preserve several long-standing principles and values in Western society but to fundamentally alter the means and instruments for implementing these values. We further presume, given the ambivalence of human nature and other factors, that people are capable of implementing this alteration, both

122

in principle and concretely. In short, we must seek to alter our society and its economic order in such a way that they encourage all people to fulfill their callings in life. We do not propose that people, for the sake of maintaining their own standard of living, ignore or neglect the other.

None of this is to suggest that greed and self-interest do not belong to human nature. On the contrary, they are indeed enduring and obstinate. And this is precisely the point. *Why* must we *stimulate* greed and *reward* self-interest? Why must we make stirring appeals designed to awaken our own capacity for greed, appeals that occasionally even suggest that without more consumption our societal order as we now know it will die? Why do we not make appeals in the reverse direction? References to greed and other sober human traits may never legitimize the present operation of our economy, for they are incapable of providing directives for a responsible economic practice. The science of economics has been far too comfortable with these anthropological assumptions or premises. And we appeal to them far too easily as a basis for rejecting any proposal to transform our approach to economic ends and means

Objection 2: What about Government Deficits?

A second objection voiced against renewing our economy is that government finances cannot tolerate a slowdown in economic growth. Currently, massive budget deficits plague the governments of the affluent nations; and if economic growth slumps, so the argument goes, then inevitably government income will decline and government deficits will rise even further. Consequently, whether we like it or not, we have no choice but to pursue economic growth.

This objection plays into a parallel argument that the economics of enough scenario sketched in Chapter 5 will weaken the competitive position of industry, because the costs of environmental and social care will increase.

The government deficit objection appears entirely plausible on the surface — until we observe that, ironically, a single critical issue has been entirely omitted. For how on earth is it possible that precisely the government budgets of the *wealthy* nations have become burdened with enormous deficits? One would expect that, surrounded by wealth, our governments would have received enough money to manage their affairs well. Why then has this not occurred? And why do deficits appear to skyrocket even under governments "committed" to deficit reduction?

There are three major reasons for the perpetual swelling of government deficits, reasons that bring us to the nub of that economic malaise known as the "crisis of the welfare state." The first reason, briefly alluded to in Chapter 2, is that government activities, such as providing police protection, administering justice, and overseeing education, health, and social welfare, belong not to the industrial but to the service sector of society. Government services are therefore susceptible to the patterns of the labor and industrial paradoxes. As we observed in Chapter 2, in the service sector productivity per worker rises more slowly than in the industrial sector. An educator cannot teach increasing numbers of students every year. Yet as an employer, the government must contend each year with rising wage and salary levels, levels that the productivity increases attainable in the advanced sectors of the economy generally dictate. Each year, therefore, most government services become proportionately more expensive than goods produced in the directly productive sector, because the wage and salary increases claimed by government-funded services and government employees cannot be recouped through higher productivity. Government income must therefore rise regularly at a *disproportionate* level if the government is to prevent deficits from escalating beyond their present state. But a society overcome by a general feeling of scarcity will hardly permit tax increase proposals much chance of success. On the contrary, most people in such a society shun taxes and attempt to roll them back whenever possible. As a result, the government increasingly finds itself in a deficit position.

A related development forms a second major reason for the alarmingly rapid increase of government deficits. Because everything in the private sector orients itself to increasing productivity and saving costs, we roll over to the government more and more expenditures and liabilities that industry itself had borne and ought to bear. These range from cultural and environmental protection to retraining and battling unemployment. Companies freely lay people off whenever they need to save costs, but as economist John Maurice Clark observed seventy years ago, the overall costs of these layoffs enter society as a whole as "social overhead costs" when unemployment benefits fall short of adequately sustaining the families involved.[1] Environmental costs and liabilities experience a similar rollover. Though the tasks of preventing and fighting environmental damage belong to all producers and consumers, by and large both producers and consumers prefer to expel them from their own areas of responsibility. The government must then attempt to remediate that which is yet remediable, often at extremely high costs.

As a result, more and more costs and liabilities press themselves upon the government, including higher costs for medical care, costs driven up by modern prosperity diseases. Together, social, environmental, and health care costs have helped to jack up government expenditures to heights hitherto unforeseen.

But there is a third significant reason for the soaring government deficits of the industrialized nations. Most levels of government social assistance and remediation expenditures are inextricably coupled with rising income levels in society in general. The Dutch secretary general of economic affairs, Professor Geelhoed, wrote in a 1991 New Year's article in the journal *Economic Statistical Reports* that each real income increase of .5 percent in collective labor agreements brings with it extra government expenditures of three billion guilders over three years. This amount is substantially higher than what the government would have received from a .5 percent hike in income taxes. This general pattern applies across the industrialized nations. As a result, the budget deficits of our Western governments deteriorate with each round of income increases.

For these three simple reasons the argument that we need economic growth in order to rehabilitate government finances is a pure fallacy, a fallacy that obscures the real problem. Yet it is an argument that is gratuitously made and uncritically accepted. In the short term, of course, economic growth does ease the problem of government finances, because higher growth means an expanded tax base. But in the long term that same growth generates significantly more government expenditures than before, especially when the general level of income in society rises to the same degree.

We must therefore turn the argument on its head. As we saw earlier, in the economics of enough we reorient our economic goals to

---

1. John Maurice Clark, *Studies in the Economics of Overhead Costs* (Chicago: University Press, 1923).

create more opportunities *within* industry for people to devote care to others and to the environment, as well as to the quality of work. We will then *prevent* further environmental and other deterioration and escalation of the costs associated with them. Further, this need not threaten the competitive position of industry; on the contrary, it is the present budget deficit positions of our governments that in principle now seriously harm the competitive position of industry. It is precisely when various differentiated sectors of society show signs of implementing *precare* on the one hand and of flattening out general wage and salary increases on the other hand that we will have opened up prospects for a *lasting* resolution to our increasingly bitter government deficit debates. For no longer would the range of the government's affairs need to expand endlessly. Indeed, where society relaxes its pattern of expelling social and environmental burdens onto the government and at the same time holds constant the salary component of government expenditures, there we will have created a durable foundation upon which to rehabilitate and renew government finances.

Objection 3: What about the Role of Government in Shaping Such a Complex Society?

In discussions of the alleviation of injustice, poverty, and violence in society, the role of government quickly assumes center stage. In today's context, such discussions also often include debate on whether or not we can really "shape" today's complex society.

While a few people today believe that the government must play no role in economic life, even fewer people defend the position that the government must guide the entire economy. This means that the discussion quickly devolves onto the degree or the extent of government involvement in alleviating distress. But too often, in our view, such discussions suffer from abstraction. We recommend instead assessing concrete local and global realities themselves, and from this assessment then determining the role or scope of government involvement. We find the debate about whether or not we can actually "shape" our society similarly abstract and unhelpful, because modern society already carries all the trademarks of being continually shaped. The key questions are rather *who* shapes *what* and on behalf of *whom?*

Let us illustrate this with the issue of technology. Technology significantly influences all of us, but especially people who work in a factory. Without being able to exercise influence on technological development, the factory worker confronts on a daily basis the consequences of "technological innovation": loss of jobs and of the quality of work. In this context, one does not often consider the possibility of shaping the workplace to be an option; yet in fact the workplace is thoroughly shaped on an ongoing basis: the employer continually shapes the workplace in such a way that it makes more profit. For the entrepreneur, today's economic order rewards his or her own self-interest and ongoing profit. He or she therefore shapes the workplace under the constraints of an extremely narrow perspective.

If one uses the phrase "shaping society" to mean regulating society by way of government subsidies, premiums, and taxes, then clearly the government's current potential for shaping society has limits. To give another example: attempts to stimulate housing construction by way of subsidies or tax breaks often do lead to the construction of new houses, but the new dwellings tend to house the privileged and prominent much more than the people in our society who have the most critical housing needs. But we may not generalize from such flaws and omissions in government policy to assert that government regulation cannot help to shape society. Instead, we must correct the flaws. The government remains an important body for helping to change society, but government regulations are effective only if a healthy majority of the population supports the need for and the sense of the regulations in question.

Meanwhile, those who argue for setting in motion the free play of social forces also seek to shape society, but their shaping does not always have positive social effects. Inevitably, setting these forces in motion results in the scope of freedom becoming smaller and smaller. Historically, when a society gives social forces free reign, the relationship between the rich and the poor develops in such a way that freedom for all perpetually diminishes.

We must therefore shape society toward an entirely different perspective. And what the shaping of society requires involves more than pleading for a change of heart in society at large. It also involves the government. Though it proceeds from the belief that people are willing to change, clearly people, including those who exercise economic power, have not always shown such a willingness. Because those who exercise economic power do not always pursue justice, we cannot avoid the use of legislation to help shape society toward a responsible economic practice. Some may argue that new consolidations of power may then emerge, but this objection may never stand in the way of change.

Shaping society also requires more than adopting a change in life-style. In and of itself, a life-style change cannot break the "logic of capitalist expansion" described in the previous chapters. Adopting elements of a new life-style does have significance, because it publicly expresses our desire to break away from existing economic patterns and power relationships. But if we renounce the pursuit of material prosperity or the appearance of more prosperity without also changing current disparities in the exercise of economic power, we will have little effect. Our experience teaches us that we cannot solve macro-economic problems by merely appealing for changes in the micro-economic sphere, because such an appeal does not fully address the current wielding of economic control.

We therefore need to locate new ways of democratizing important decisions about investments and their financing. In the framework of a responsible society, at minimum this implies that those who wield economic power must become more accountable for the decisions they make. The right of people to own and participate in the significant decisions affecting their lives deserves much broader attention in economics. We must seek *mutual* responsibility. And we must explore avenues for enhancing mutual responsibility, such as pursuing local community economic development and giving mutual responsibility more emphasis in child and adult education.

Unquestionably, the abuse of economic power will continue to raise its ugly head in society. But we reject the thesis that it must have the final word. Instead, we advocate an economy that presents fewer opportunities to abuse power.

Does it make sense to argue for a different economic approach when such enormous power is wielded in today's economy? We acknowledge the scope of that power. Yet we believe that we can seek to alter existing power structures only after having acquired insight into how these structures work. This, of course, does not excuse any of us from concretely seeking different power relationships. But doing so becomes easier when we possess a clear perspective on an alternative. We must then think through and present recommendations for change. And we shall broach several such recommendations in the final chapter.

Objection 4: What about Population Growth?

World population growth is discouraging for all who pursue a better situation for the victims of today's global economic system. Population increases aggravate their difficulties. The significant and historically unprecedented explosion of production after World War II has remained largely invisible because we must divide the total production over so many more people. From the vantage point of alleviating poverty, health problems, and environmental damage, the rapid rise in world population, especially in the Third World, is truly disturbing.

Many people object to the possibility of regulating birth as well as death. Of course, we consider this area primarily the responsibility of parents. But responsibility also rests on private-sector institutions and governments to provide parents with as much help as possible. Do we in the West do everything we can to inform and educate parents? And have our churches done so?

To arrive at a balanced view of population growth, we must consider the responsibilities of the industrialized nations themselves. On average each inhabitant of the industrialized nations consumes about ten times more energy and resources than each inhabitant of the nations of the South. Seventy-five percent of "greenhouse gas" emissions come from 25 percent of the world's population, and the large majority of that 25 percent inhabit the North. This, as we shall see, plays into the startling population explosion in the Third World.

Financial support to the United Nations Fund for Population Activities (UNFPA) ought to be bolstered by larger contributions from member states. New studies of the UNFPA show that family planning programs require more resources to continue. This is confirmed by the *Report of the Women's Congress for a Healthy Planet,* which estimates that approximately 500 million couples would participate in family planning programs if they had the resources to do so.[2]

In the meantime, however, poverty *itself* increasingly causes rapid population growth in the Third World. In the context of Africa, the *Hunger 1992* report states the matter precisely: "While security in old age for both men and women wholly depends on their surviving children, most Africans will continue to want large families. . . . In

2. November 1991.

the absence of greater access to more education and higher status for girls and women, early marriage and frequent child-bearing will continue."[3] The primary population growth initiative therefore must come by way of alleviating poverty, in combination with efforts to improve the position of women in the economy, in education, and in society as a whole.[4]

Objection 5: Is Not Economic Renewal Idealist and Utopian?

Opponents of the renewal of economic theory and practice repeatedly accuse those who promote it of being idealist, if not utopian. They counter with "realism." But what does their realism refer to? Usually, it seems that "realism" refers to the assumed inability of people to change as well as to the complexity of modern society. But we use the word "realism" to refer to "reality," especially the horrific reality we attempted to sketch in the first chapter. We do not pretend that our proposals will simply dissolve this reality, but we do submit that their implementation will help to alleviate the suffering, injustice, and violence which that reality brings, and eventually bring it to a halt. We consider it unrealistic and even illusory to think that the economy can simply continue to develop along its current antiquated patterns, while we remain oblivious to the consequences for people and the environment. In the words of United States Vice President Al Gore, "It is as

3. Bread for the World Institute on Hunger and Development, *Hunger 1992* (Washington, D.C., 1991), 34.

4. In *Earth in the Balance* (New York: Houghton Mifflin Company, 1992), Al Gore describes a population growth "success story": "One of the most interesting case studies of demographic transition in the Third World comes from the Kerala province of southwestern India, where population growth has stabilized at zero even though per capita incomes are still extremely low. The provincial leaders, with assistance from international population funding, developed a plan that is keyed to Kerala's unique cultural, social, religious, and political characteristics and focuses on a few crucial factors. First, they have achieved an extremely high rate of literacy, especially among women. Second, through good health care and adequate nutrition, they have lowered their infant mortality dramatically. And third, they have made birth control readily and freely available. The consequences are little short of remarkable: in an area of the world characterized by uncontrollable population growth, Kerala's rate more nearly resembles that of Sweden than nearby Bombay" (313).

if the ultrarational 'economic man' of classical theory actually believes in magic."[5]

But another factor comes into play here. We can no longer remain blind to the consequences of our economic actions, because increasingly they recoil upon us. Their harmful effects conflict with a just, sustainable, and participatory society. What, then, are people capable of in a participatory process? Is it "realistic" to expect that people will orient themselves to others? Though they may not, they also *may*.

We endorse the approach unpacked twenty-five years ago by Dutch thinker Feitse Boerwinkel and by Dr. Martin Luther King, Jr. In a book entitled *Inclusive Thinking,* Boerwinkel argues that our dominant mode of thinking is antagonistic: "We think in terms of 'either/or': 'either he goes, or I go. Either his business succeeds, or mine does.' People have therefore always been inclined to group together for the purpose of opposing other groups of people."[6] Forms of cooperation also exist in antagonistic thinking, but they are limited; they assist one group in opposing another group.

Antagonistic or exclusive thinking has been imparted to all of us. But if we extend this mode of thinking into today's global political and economic relationships, then we raise the prospects of mutual annihilation. With exclusive thinking, we can no longer win wars, for example; we can only engage in mutual destruction.

Boerwinkel argues that we must adopt new modes of thinking. He contends that a new mode of thinking, also in economics, will lead to new action. To this end, he contrasts *inclusive* thinking with exclusive or antagonistic thinking. Inclusive thinking "proceeds fundamentally from the point of view that my well-being cannot be gained at the expense of the other. I can have it only if at the same time I advance the well-being of the other." Significantly, Boerwinkel adds: "One must not construe this statement as idealist, but as realist. Its intention is not to suggest that it is more noble or nice to advance the well-being of the other, but that it is more sensible."

In his last book, *Where Do We Go from Here: Chaos or Community?,* Martin Luther King eloquently develops the identical point:

5. Ibid., 187.

6. Feitse Boerwinkel, *Inclusief Denken: een Andere Tijd Vraagt een Ander Denken* [Inclusive Thinking: A Different Age Calls for Different Thinking], 18th ed. (Bussum: Unieboek, 1975).

From time immemorial men have lived by the principle that "self-preservation is the first law of life." But this is a false assumption. I would say that other-preservation is the first law of life. It is the first law of life precisely because we cannot preserve self without being concerned about preserving other selves. The universe is so structured that things go awry if men are not diligent in their cultivation of the other-regarding dimension. "I" cannot reach fulfillment without "thou."[7]

Significantly, King adds:

A genuine program on the part of the wealthy nations to make prosperity a reality for the poor nations will in the final analysis enlarge the prosperity of all. One of the best proofs that reality hinges on moral foundations is the fact that when men and governments work devotedly for the good of others, they achieve their own enrichment in the process.[8]

Inclusive thinking, which seeks to serve the common good, forms a strong part of many of our traditions. In *Habits of the Heart,* their survey and assessment of American values, Robert Bellah and his colleagues find that an emphasis on the common good lies at the heart of "the biblical and republican traditions" of the United States.[9] They write:

We have committed what to the founders of our nation was the cardinal sin: we have put our own good, as individuals, as groups, as a nation, ahead of the common good. . . . Jefferson was appalled at the enormous wealth and miserable poverty that he found in France and was sanguine about [America's] future as a free people only because we lacked such extremes.[10]

---

7. In Martin Luther King, Jr., *A Testament of Hope: The Essential Writings of Martin Luther King Jr.,* ed. James Melvin Washington (San Francisco: Harper & Row, 1986), 625.

8. Ibid.

9. Robert N. Bellah et al., *Habits of the Heart: Individualism and Commitment in American Life* (Berkeley: University of California Press, 1985).

10. Ibid., 285.

Based on these and other arguments, we contend that inclusive thinking both has historical roots and is in principle realistic.

Objection 6: Are Not the Issues International in Nature?

A final objection frequently voiced against those who propose change in the economy is that today's major economic problems have become international, and that as a result single nations, or even states or provinces within a nation, are too insignificant to accomplish anything on their own. In most cases, however, this argument acts as a foil for refusing to consider proposals for renewal on the basis of their own merits. By simply deferring to the power of other countries, people conveniently sidestep the need for self-reflection and eventual change in economic behavior.

Of course, in many respects nations do find themselves dependent upon outside economic influences. But it would be incorrect to assume that these make up the sole economic influences. Ironically, those who observe discussions under way in even more "powerless" countries about implementing an alternative economic practice come away impressed by the wide variety of economic activities and alternatives. It is our ardent desire that all of us, whether inhabitants of superpower or nonsuperpower states in the West, participate more fully in such activities, in order to help build up an international network of those who wish to give people and nations the opportunity to meet their genuine needs and to face the future without fear.

In the context of renewing the economy, we must not tolerate appeals to the fact that our particular nation is not an island and thus cannot act alone, appeals that serve to dismiss any call to amend our current political and economic order. We must also emphatically reject any assertion that because we criticize our current political and economic order, we belong by definition in the camp of those internationally who promote the centrally planned economy. Such black-and-white thinking, which we repeatedly encounter, is shortsighted, unfruitful, and false.

CHAPTER 8

A Twelve-Step Program for Economic Recovery

In this final chapter we shall explore the possibilities of taking a few steps *now* toward a renewed economy. New thinking about economics requires new action. In today's context, renewing the economy toward an economy of care requires nothing less than a conversion.[1] Conversion means making a 180-degree turn, or making a revolution. The word "revolution" accurately describes the radicality and all-embracing change we believe is required. But as a description of the *means* of change, "revolution" is far less suitable. For a revolution as we understand it today in the West would destroy not only the prerequisites of life but also the objectives of an economy of care.

What we need is a prophetic openness, in the sense of the biblical prophets who startle and arouse us to action, combined with infinite patience and inventiveness in stimulating change toward the common

---

1. Years ago the German philosopher Ernst Bloch wrote about Christians: "When you begin to pay in hard cash for what you have preached about — the poor, the exploited and the oppressed — then you are Christians. If you do not, then you are chatter-boxes and hypocrites." Can we achieve something of the radicality of human action to which the Bible calls us, also in economics? Does not the call to conversion in today's context include a call for societal transformation? For has not the economy as it presently operates had a devastating impact on Christianity?

It is our conviction that the Christian community has paid too little attention to these questions. Perhaps the tension between the reality of life and the reality of God is so poignant that we hastily resign ourselves to doing something different on Monday than what we have committed ourselves to on Sunday.

good. And we must operate from an accurate assessment of the power that today's sociopolitical and economic order wields.

In this chapter we shall formulate a twelve-step program for economic recovery. As we do so, we shall focus not on meeting "infinite needs" but on building human relationships that possess less injustice, violence, and oppression than they do now. The twelve steps proposed here are partly negative (that is, they outline what we must abandon and alleviate), but largely positive.

They are also intimately related. To best grasp their interrelationship, let us juxtapose for a moment images depicting two types of societies: a tunnel society and a fruit tree society.[2]

Consider a traffic tunnel and a fruit tree. They are similar in the sense that processes flow through each of them. Each also performs a function and has an objective. However, the consequences of each process are strikingly different. In a tunnel, traffic must travel through as quickly and as safely as possible and then depart out the other end; traffic must reach the light at the end of the tunnel. However, in order to achieve a maximal flow of traffic, only those vehicles suitable for tunnel traffic are welcome in the tunnel. Some, because of size for example, are excluded at the tunnel's entrance. Then, once vehicles have entered, the trip through the tunnel requires them to maintain a minimum speed; otherwise the din and accumulation of exhaust and other pollutants become unbearable.

By contrast, the fruit tree operates under a different flow principle. A fruit tree utilizes the cooperation of every cell in order to blossom and bear fruit. But this, too, has consequences: the fruit tree will never scale the height of heaven. Every fruit tree displays the built-in "wisdom" to stop growing in height at a particular moment. From that moment forward, the tree directs its maturation efforts toward the production of fruit instead.

The juxtaposition speaks for itself. In principle, the trademark of a tunnel society is a ceaseless expansion of production and productivity, the purpose of which is to transport us to the light at the end of the tunnel: a rising standard of living, along with a substantial

2. Economist A. B. Cramp of Cambridge University was the first to use the metaphor of a "tunnel society," supported by a "tunnel vision," to describe our contemporary society. See A. B. Cramp, *Notes Towards a Christian Critique of Secular Economic Theory* (Toronto: Institute for Christian Studies, 1975), 62.

enough increase in prosperity to permit us to fund environmental protection, social and medical care, and development aid for poor countries. But entering and maintaining the process of the tunnel require "sacrifices." Because some people do not have the capacity to work as efficiently as others, they are *excluded* from the production process. Some become unemployed; others, such as some who are physically or developmentally challenged, cannot handle the demands of the production process. Likewise, maintaining the process of the tunnel requires *expulsion*. Because increased efficiency requires us to ignore the persistent demands of the environment and of people who have been ostracized, in a tunnel economy we find it necessary to expel environmental and social burdens onto other sectors of society, including the state. We do so because we consider it imperative that the process of the tunnel continue. Finally, the tunnel process requires *extraction*. In a competitive climate, business finds it necessary to extract as much as possible from the services that land, labor, and capital provide. But this extraction gives rise to the need for society to remedy the distress caused by unemployment, environmental destruction, and workplace stress.

The tunnel society is therefore a postcare society. Strikingly, addressing the needs that the tunnel process *itself* creates — the needs of all that have been excluded, expelled, and extracted — is now significantly reducing economic expansion and raising deficits in our society. Indeed, so much is this the case that, rather than entering the daylight at the end of the tunnel, we sense that we are racing faster and faster in a tunnel that is *elongating* instead. With a kind of tunnel vision, we then appeal for *more* production to finance *more* postcare expenditures. But now suddenly the possibility looms that, because our society's critical needs are escalating at an unprecedented rate, and because scarcity is rapidly becoming more and more generalized, the tunnel is becoming a closed loop. Perhaps we will continue to produce and produce, but the promised prosperity will never arrive. *Scarcity* will arrive instead.

Throughout this book, in contrast to the tunnel society perspective, we have advocated embracing an economic wisdom that is reminiscent of the "wisdom" displayed by the fruit tree. A tree society is a precare society. After reaching its optimal height, the tree society redirects its maturation processes toward bearing fruit for others: it seeks to provide sufficient opportunities for meaningful work, for the meeting of basic material needs both at home and around the world, for environmental sustainability for ourselves and for future generations, and for the preservation of noncommercialized art and culture. A precare economy *includes* rather than excludes people; it *internalizes* and *takes responsibility* for its effects rather than expels them to other sectors of society; and it *practices restraint* and *replenishes* rather than extracts.

But this, too, has consequences. To implement a precare economy, our society must exercise the wisdom to slow down and eventually stop its endless material expansion and redirect its maturation energies toward the production of fruit instead.

The twelve steps that follow are thus designed to help redirect our tunnel economy to a tree economy. They are designed to help put today's economy on track. While some of the steps build upon each other, others take quite different directions toward the economic and societal conversion required.

Step 1: Renewing the World Monetary System

Injustice lies at the very heart of today's international monetary system. As we saw in Chapter 4, the injustice lies especially in this fact: the making of international liquidities, or those forms of money used in international trade and payment transfers, lies exclusively in the hands of the affluent countries. Their currencies serve as the generally acceptable means of payment in the international exchange, and their "votes" tip the scales inside the International Monetary Fund (IMF). Their "special drawing rights" (SDR's) contribute directly to the growth of international money supply. The distribution of voting rights in the IMF is regulated in such a way that the countries with the highest incomes per capita and the highest exports have the largest influence in IMF decisions. It has been said, using an entirely incorrect reference to the words of Jesus in the Gospel of Matthew, that a "Matthew principle" operates within the IMF: to those who have, much will be given; from those who have little, even that will be taken away.

The wealthy nations have used their preferential position in the world money economy to vigorously promote their own interests. Without this preferential position the United States could never have sustained its long-standing annual balance-of-payments deficit, a deficit that year after year lies in the billions of dollars. This amounts to permitting itself to tread in dangerously oversized shoes at the expense of the rest of the world. But it must also be said that the wealthy nations have not responsibly managed the world money economy, because together they generated a far greater increase in the quantity of currencies than was necessary. As we noted earlier, a shocking sign of this mismanagement is the reality that the amount of international liquidities now circulating in the "pure" financial circuit is *thirty to forty* times that which circulates in the so-called real circuit of money used directly in the buying and selling of goods and services. In the face of this tidal wave of money created by the wealthy nations, it is no wonder that it is virtually impossible to protect rates of exchange from speculation. The world monetary system has gone adrift; it is at the mercy of the torrent of uncoordinated and uncontrolled capital movements around the world. Here, too, in the light of this gross mismanagement, renewal is urgently required.

But it is precisely at this point that the possibility of renewal opens up, the possibility of adopting a course that helps to repair the fundamental injustices done to the poor nations. By no means is it necessary or a kind of "natural law" that the wealthy nations must hold a monopoly over world money supply. In the 1970s, several people, among them Robert Triffin, formulated far-reaching proposals designed to give the special drawing rights of the IMF more stature in the world monetary system. Triffin and others proposed new rules for the distribution of special drawing rights under which poor nations would receive direct access to a reasonable amount of new international currency creation. Adopting such rules, they argued, would accelerate the process by which the poor nations were paying off their existing debts, but it would also begin the process of allowing them to build up their own prosperity, step by step.

Proposals such as these, however, have consistently met with a loud objection. For if such a proposal is to succeed, then the wealthy nations must retard their *own* creation of key currencies. Otherwise, the increase in currency would simply cause general world inflation. And it is precisely the unwillingness of the wealthy nations to relinquish some of their currency privileges that has caused them, time and time again, to reject critically needed proposals for reform. For not only would the wealthy nations lose some of their power, but they would also retard the rise in their own material prosperity.

Yet now more than ever change is both essential and unavoidable. We may not allow the matter to rest any longer. We must cut to the quick of the deepening and endless international cycle of impoverishment and enrichment.

Therefore, our first concrete step toward economic renewal is the proposal that *one or more of the wealthy nations holding voting rights in the International Monetary Fund declare their willingness to reduce the relative weight of their own vote and share for the benefit of the vote and share of the bloc of the world's poorest so-called low-income countries.*

This step would be more effective if it became linked to the proposal to institute a special distribution round of several billion special drawing rights designed specifically for debt redemption by the world's poorest nations. Not only would this create a rare feeling of relief in sub-Saharan Africa, where there is now so much suffering, but it would also help to teach the affluent nations of the North to discipline their excessive discharge of money over the world year after year. It would go a long way toward a structural solution to the present world monetary imbalance.

Step 2: Wage and Salary Increases

Proposals such as the one outlined above depend on more than the goodwill of one or more governments. Even the best political intentions can founder on a lack of willingness within society as a whole. In the imagery introduced at the beginning of this chapter, if society itself shows no inclination or desire to redirect its maturation energies away from sheer expansion and toward precare, then a government cannot move forward with a new policy. In other words, if a society does not wish to contribute to better precare for people, culture, and the environment — precisely by using income and consumption desires as a means to reaching this end — then the government has little room to move. This leads us to a proposal that we address to both business and labor, namely, *that they expressly broaden their individual and collective tasks to provide precare for people and the environment, satisfying work, and the production of as responsible an end product as possible, in exchange for increases in real income and profits; and that, wherever possible, they do so in mutual cooperation.* Practically, this can take the form of, among other things, the establishment of *directed funds,* funds made possible by the curtailment of wages and/or profits.

The backdrop of this proposal is that general wage and salary increases make endemic all of the shadow sides of our current economic order, as we have explained. Pressure on people intensifies, because salary increases allow industry to boost its claim to their buying power; pressure on the environment escalates, because every further increase in consumption implies more use of raw materials and energy; pressure on transductive labor, which devotes care to humanity and the environment, heightens because of our increasing inability to pay for it; and, in the framework of the global economy, pressure on the poor intensifies because they have less opportunity to gain access to their land and its scarce resources. In other words, general wage and salary hikes make the three critical problems with which we began unmistakably larger. General wage and salary increases cause people to price themselves, the environment, and other human beings out of the market. Because of this, the market will become more and more turbulent as time goes on.

As an alternative to the prevailing growth emphases of management and labor, we recommend instead a policy that promotes a broader distribution of available labor. We do not mean that certain *specific* groups of people, namely, people who cannot meet their basic needs, including recipients of inadequate government benefits, ought not to receive wage and salary increases. But in the light of what we have seen in this book, we reject the suggestion that we must achieve general across-the-board wage and salary hikes to restore the economy.

Rather, together we must learn to consciously "open" the economy to the basic subsistence needs that now do not enter the market, needs that have care for other people and the environment at their center. For unions, this means that they may stake claim to the *full* amount of surplus available in the so-called advanced sector of the economy. But they must also — in consultation with their members — be prepared to earmark this surplus not primarily for salary increases but for a number of concrete funds or objectives. Such funds would have as their purpose the creation and expansion of jobs, but jobs located in designated fields of *care*, fields that now are either neglected or abandoned. Examples include the following:

1. creating a fund for improving the quality of work (such as unions have done in Sweden for a number of years);
2. creating an employment fund to combat urban decay;

140

3. creating an employment fund to help alleviate poverty with appropriate technology;
4. creating an employment fund for preserving the environment and saving energy;
5. creating a conversion fund to assist in the changeover from wartime to peacetime production.

We appreciate that this proposal lays a great deal on the plate of trade unions and that it leans heavily on the willingness of union members. Nevertheless, it is by no means unrealistic or even outside of the realm of what is currently being done. Let us consider in more detail several of the examples introduced in Chapter 5. In the fall of 1992 the president of the large Dutch Christian Labor Union (CNV), Anton Westerlaken, proposed to freeze real wage increases for a minimum of five years if such a freeze would lead to more jobs, more care for the natural environment, and improvements in the work environment. Westerlaken's proposal has met with widespread support both within and outside CNV membership, and it may well open up new forms of cooperation between management and labor in the Netherlands. Similarly, the largest industrial labor union in western Germany, I-G Metall, has offered to freeze real wages for five years in exchange for more jobs, especially in the eastern part of Germany.

Likewise, in Quebec a Solidarity Fund has operated under the auspices of the Quebec Federation of Labour since 1982. Quebec citizens can invest moneys in the fund, and these are matched by a 20 percent tax deduction from the provincial government and a further 20 percent tax deduction from the federal government. These moneys are then invested in small to medium-sized businesses that are relatively labor-intensive. Further, recognizing the debilitating effects of technological innovation on employment, the fund invests in technological development only selectively, with a view toward the overall effect of the technology in question on employment. The general consensus is that the Solidarity Fund has made a tangible contribution to maintaining employment levels in Quebec. More recently, under the auspices of the Canadian Federation of Labour, similar funds (such as the Working Ventures Fund in Ontario) have been established in most Canadian provinces, with the same tax backing from both the provincial and federal governments.

While none of these funds has yet specifically embraced the

objectives of environmental responsibility, the need for a socially responsible product, or the need to instrumentalize income levels for the purposes of precare, in our view they represent a significant step in the right direction. And these limitations, too, may change: in an address delivered in Toronto, a Canadian representative of the United Steelworkers of America argued that "from our point of view, exploring new forms of corporate structure and capital investment is as much an obligation of a responsible trade union in these times as our normal bargaining and advocacy." He suggested further:

> Rooted in their own homes and communities, worker-owners will have a greater sense of proprietorship over their enterprise, will be sensitive to environmental impacts, and to the constant need to upgrade quality and add value, and to upgrade their own skills. Workers who have a stake in their place of work will undoubtedly have a long-term perspective regarding their investment.[3]

Proposals such as these may still, however, appear entirely new in many contexts. Because we appreciate that they ask a great deal of labor unions, and because much rides on this proposal, we shall add a couple of brief remarks.

First, people will relinquish general salary increases much more readily if they not only accept the reasons for doing so but also have a say in what will be done with their resources. Unions ought therefore to locate these funds at a decentralized level, such as in an industrial sector, or even within a specific organization or firm. This will bring the added benefit of qualitatively strengthening union partnership from "below."

Secondly, workers can earmark funds for specific cooperative firms or organizations, such as North American counterparts of the Dutch MEMO companies, companies that are not primarily designed for profit and that, through their governing constitutions, help to renew the control structure of society toward broader participation and care.

Thirdly, planning and erecting such experiments will help to create a new energy in society, an energy perhaps comparable to the energy

---

3. Unpublished address (delivered at Beyond Foodbanks conference, Toronto, February 15, 1993), 11-12.

created when postwar Europe took up the task of rebuilding itself, despite the substantial built-in investment restrictions of the time.

Step 3: Structuring Precare

Appealing to industry to expressly open itself up to notions of responsibility that are broader than that of producing products for the market as efficiently and as inexpensively as possible is made problematic by the lack of flexibility available to industry. National and international competition is stiff and harsh, leaving little room for risky ventures, even if commitments have been made from within society to slacken pressure for wage and salary increases. Here again we encounter a problem of societal order or structure. Not only does society itself not promote such initiatives, but it can even ruthlessly punish them. How then can the social context behind the development of a more responsible company change from negative to positive?

George Goyder, in his books *The Responsible Company* and *The Just Enterprise,* has reflected on this very issue.[4] And it is from him that we derive our third step: *in order to encourage a company to adopt a broader range of objectives, it ought to become eligible to receive the legally sanctioned title "Responsible Company" (or a similar title), a title that could assist the company in acquiring a loyal and steady clientele.*

Practically, this could be regulated in such a way that the joint recommendation by at least one labor union committed to broader precare objectives, one sustainable agriculture or environmental organization, and one consumer body would make a company or firm eligible to receive the legally protected title "Responsible Company." The public would expect that the organizations nominating such companies had done so because they had observed the company in question demonstrating exceptional *precare* for the environment, for its employees, and for the production of a socially responsible product. A regular review process and a complaint procedure would also need to be in place. Part of the appeal of this proposal is that, though designed to stimulate corporate responsibility, indirectly it would help to mobilize consumer responsibility. It would encourage consumers

4. George Goyder, *The Responsible Company* (Oxford: Basil Blackwell, 1961); idem, *The Just Enterprise* (London: A. Deutsch, 1987).

at the point of purchase to base their buying decisions on more factors than price and design alone. It would also encourage the establishment of new companies committed to change, companies that together would form the vanguard of the renewal required for our economy to become an economy of precare.

A related suggestion, while more limited in scope because it addresses only the start-up of new companies, has even deeper ramifications. In *Habits of the Heart,* Robert Bellah and his colleagues argue for a "reassertion of the idea that incorporation is a concession of public authority to a private group in return for service to the public good."[5] With this suggestion they link the right of establishing new, larger companies to the legal form of the limited liability company, by which people within society at large are best suited to determine whether or not certain *responsibilities* are inherent in the *right* of incorporation. Bellah and his coauthors suggest that any such "concession" to incorporation made by the public should occur only on the basis of well-formulated conditions, including effective public accountability. This would "change what is now called the 'social responsibility of the corporation' from its present status, where it is often a kind of public relations whipped cream decorating the corporate pudding, to a constitutive element in the corporation itself. This, in turn, would involve a fundamental alteration in the role and training of the manager. Management would become a profession in the older sense of the word."[6]

We support this proposal, especially if it also applies to company mergers that overstep an appropriate scale and to other forms of corporate concentration. This proposal would then focus more attention on the legal structure governing the founding of new or amalgamated companies.

Step 4: Reorienting the Structure of Price and Production

Throughout this book, we have attempted to show not only that our society has reached the point where it must be renewed but also that

---

5. Robert Bellah et al., *Habits of the Heart* (Berkeley: University of California Press, 1985), 290.
6. Ibid.

the matter of renewal belongs on the agenda of our society as a whole. Relying simply on government measures is entirely inadequate.

However, this does not mean that society is capable of accomplishing renewal independently of government. For renewal to be successful, government policy must encourage rather than discourage it. And Steps 4 through 7 specifically address how government policy can encourage the renewal of our society.

Though it is rare, occasionally elements within the governments of the West entertain the possibility of structuring their fiscal policies "selectively" to enhance social and environmental sustainability. When push comes to shove, however, in virtually every instance this form of "selectivity" falls off of the table. When governments grant financial incentives or impose levies on businesses, they seldom do so with a view to care for the environment, the conservation of energy, or the labor-intensiveness and quality of work; rather, they almost always do so with a view to increasing production and productivity. Lack of responsible "selectivity" in the government's incentive structure negatively affects the three economic impasses flagged in this book. What is also striking is that when government policies speak of "innovation," they almost exclusively mean that which is required to expand production so that our industrial system reaches full capacity. Almost never do government policies use "innovation" to refer to that which improves our ability to provide adequate care for people and the environment, or that which places technology in the service of precare, or the prevention of harm or damage. "Large scale" remains a key phrase in government policy. Ironically, this phrase also evokes the image of a large-scale and all-embracing government, which, seemingly of its own accord, becomes the natural but inevitable partner of large industry.

In contrast, there are ways of permitting government policy to encourage social, ecological, and energy sustainability at both local and global levels. Various governments and research bodies have provided detailed examples, with calculations showing their economic effects, of using taxes and subsidies (in particular the goods and services tax) to encourage companies to clean the environment, produce labor-intensively, and conserve energy, while simultaneously slowing down the production of companies that do the exact opposite. We do not view this as an "unnatural" interference in the "natural" operation of the market. On the contrary, because the market is by "nature" oblivious to the future of the environment and to the well-being of future generations, it is the natural role of a government that seeks to do justice and serve the common good to bring the price structure in line with society's long-term responsibilities. Low fuel prices, for instance, may conform with today's market forces, but when seen from the vantage point of future generations, they encourage massive waste of a highly scarce and basic resource.

We must add the rider that a policy of attaching "prices" to external effects by fining those who contaminate the soil and pollute the air and water does not do the whole load of laundry, so to speak. We do not make life richer by attaching a price tag to everything. At certain key points a maintenance economy worthy of its name will halt the operation of the money economy and encourage the operation of the informal economy. Some activities, such as the improper disposal of oil, are prohibited by law. With other activities, not only must we pursue legal regulation but we must also act *before* the regulation becomes official. The threat of officially closing down a company, for example, is an appropriate means of sanction when a company steadfastly refuses to live up to its public responsibility, or to the requirements of *oikonomia,* including care for the health of people and the environment. In this respect, government policy is simply too softhearted and operates with far too little foresight. Government policy must also demonstrate that preserving our forests — if we are not too late — *takes priority* over current and future automobile use. Price signals are appropriate here, but so are automobile traffic restrictions at certain intervals, such as introducing rationing or automobile-less days, as well as imposing stiff emission requirements. For our transportation practices affect not only us: they also affect generations yet to come. People will accept unpopular measures if they cannot deny or ignore their necessity.

We must therefore introduce into the entire range of government economic policies, including its fiscal policies, the principle of social, environmental, and energy selectivity, so that government can provide a maximum contribution to the sustainability of society as a whole.

We therefore urge managing taxation policy in such a way that it encourages the implementation of an economics of care. Specifically, we urge levying a higher goods and services tax on capital-intensive and environmentally damaging products; a lower goods and services tax on environmentally friendly, labor-intensive products and activities in the service sector; and a lower goods and services tax on public transit and repairs to existing products.

Step Five: Financing Social Security

As we have noted several times, in a market economy labor increasingly prices itself out of the market. But the other reality is that labor *becomes* priced out of the market because of the actions of government and employers. The methods of financing today's social security system provide a striking illustration. As employers, employees, and citizens, we pay premiums to the government in order to provide social security benefits for other citizens now and for ourselves in the future. But because we base premiums on the number of *employees* of a company, companies and organizations deduct and forward to the government moneys only according to the volume of employees they currently maintain on payroll. The volume of personnel determines a company's or organization's social security commitment. In other words, we tax only the labor factor.

Now that social security costs have increasingly become a real burden for many companies, it is becoming more and more clear that this arrangement leads to increasingly unjust consequences. Specifically, our present system rewards the strong but penalizes the weak. Consider two companies, each with one hundred employees. The first company — say, an oil refinery — has an annual volume of 100 million dollars, and it has laid off twenty employees in the past year because of increased mechanization and automation. The second company is labor-intensive, has an annual volume of 10 million dollars, and in the past year has maintained employment at its present level. Note that the powerful capital-intensive company's social security obligation per dollar of volume is only one-tenth of the other company's. Not only that, but the capital-intensive company *reduces* its social security obligation further by laying employees off! This is both economically skewed and socially unjust. We financially reward those who work capital-intensively and automate; we financially penalize those who work labor-intensively and save jobs.

In order to maintain the main elements of our society's care and to promote justice and the growth of labor-intensive employment, we join with those who argue for cofinancing the social security system on the basis of capital strength, not just labor strength. Levying employer premiums based on the net added value of a company provides a more solid foundation for assessing employer obligations than does levying premiums based on the number of employees still working at a firm.

We must therefore fundamentally alter how we levy employer contributions to our social security system by no longer basing these contributions on the number of employees in a company but on its net added value (that is, the company's volume minus the costs of raw materials and components).

Step 6: An Innovative Environmental Policy

The studies of the Netherlands Scientific Council for Government Policy referred to in Chapter 5 show the potential social and economic benefits of implementing the economics of enough. The economics of enough scenario contains several significant outcomes, as we noted earlier. It registers better outcomes for the environment and for employment levels than do the other scenarios (namely, export-oriented growth, or expanding the market economy, and consumption-oriented growth, or enlarging the welfare state), and it generates a balance of payments surplus that allows for expanding our commitments to Third World countries. And of the three scenarios, it has the most favorable impact on today's exorbitant government deficits.

Of course, these favorable outcomes come at a price: a relatively smaller increase in general income and consumption levels than those achieved in the other two scenarios. But in the framework of the objectives of the economics of enough, this was entirely to be expected.

The policy changes required to arrive at the economics of enough scenario contain some elements that governments can implement in the relatively short term. Such changes would be designed to maintain or increase industriousness but not necessarily production growth.

The following recommendations can be implemented in the relatively short term, and they are specifically designed to encourage environmentally friendly production. If implemented, these recommendations will also bring about a substantial increase in employment. *Governments should do the following:*

148

1. *Adopt the principle not only that the polluter must pay but also that the polluter must, where possible, prevent pollution (the "prevention principle").* The accountability of every economic agent must form the heart of any society oriented toward care.
2. *Set minimum standards for the preservation of human health and the environment, standards that form the point of departure for establishing maximum standards for levels of pollution caused by the most damaging contaminants.* Governments then would use these standards to establish binding restrictions on polluters for the pollution that they cause.
3. *Alter and reverse the "selectivity" of the government's present incentive structure in agriculture to encourage farm stewardship instead of maximum production.* This would include, for example, assisting farmers in bridging the critical transition period from petrochemically-based to non-petrochemically-based, diversified production.[7]
4. *Promote more intensive recycling of waste materials as well as the development of technologies that are environmentally clean and that purify waste gases and water.*
5. *Seek improvements in housing, including the capability of dwellings to enhance community and neighborhood interaction.*
6. *Encourage expansion of the issues of environmental responsibility in the training sector, in both child and adult education.*

Finally, we encourage nature-protection and environment organizations to cooperate on specific projects. As an example, at a Rural Environmental Consultation meeting held some time ago in Holland, ten large nature-protection and environment organizations jointly agreed to invest 20 billion dollars toward fighting acid rain. In the end investments of this kind pay for themselves, thanks to a drop in energy costs, improvements in the market posi-

---

7. With respect to agriculture, note that federal funds in the United States have accounted for 20 percent to 40 percent of all farm income since 1955 (Herman E. Daly and Bernard B. Cobb, Jr., *For the Common Good* [Boston: Beacon Press, 1989], 271). By and large, the fiscal involvement of government has encouraged agribusiness and high levels of production at the expense of sustainability and stewardship. The issues, of course, are complex. But in keeping with what we have found in the overall economics of enough scenario, this alteration in incentive structure may well have the added effect of enhancing local independence and decision making and reducing the government's fiscal involvement in agriculture over time.

tion of companies that supply the equipment needed, and the prevention of additional losses of environmental values. This initiative will create 120,000 extra jobs. And the damage that acid rain causes, which is estimated at 1.5 billion dollars *annually,* will decrease substantially.

Step 7: Measuring Economic Growth

Since World War II, it has been international practice to use the gross national product (GNP) as the measure of economic success. As we alluded to in Chapter 6, it is also common knowledge that the GNP is an inadequate measure of economic growth because it does not evaluate the distribution of that product among people. For example, it is quite possible that the GNP may rise even as the real income of the lowest income group drops substantially. A dramatic rise in the incomes of the highest income groups will more than offset a drop in the income level of the lowest income groups.

It is therefore understandable that new measures have been proposed for measuring the increase or decrease of prosperity. One such measure is contained in the annual reports of the United Nations Development Program (UNDP). The UNDP Index measures not only economic growth but also human development. It factors in answers to such questions as these: What is the country's infant mortality rate? How many children are going to school? What is the degree of literacy among the people? What is the income distribution? How is land divided? The answers to these questions reveal a great deal about the welfare of a people. The reports of the UNDP also demonstrate that such indicators offer a better means of assessing the degree of progress achieved by the development process.

A second series of measurement proposals takes as its impetus the fact that the conventional GNP does not account for the social costs of production. Nowhere, for example, does the fact that the "use" value of the environment is rapidly diminishing enter the GNP calculations. But a simple truth endures, namely, that when we use up our provisions, we have not become richer.

In their convincing book *For the Common Good: Redirecting the Economy toward Community, the Environment, and a Sustainable Future,* authors Herman E. Daly and John B. Cobb, Jr., present an index for measuring sustainable welfare.[8] Their proposal contains, among other elements, a measurement and valuation of environmental damage. The results show that, since the beginning of the 1970s, economic prosperity per capita of the United States' population has scarcely increased. Taking into account the reality that the actual costs of production do not express themselves in prices, the measure demonstrates that current prosperity is illusory.

Many governments in the industrialized West have studied the possibility of using other measures than the gross national product. Our seventh step is therefore this: *we urge organizations and political parties to take steps toward introducing new public measurements of economic growth as quickly as possible. Further, we urge our governments themselves to place this issue on the agendas of the emerging North American trading bloc, the Group of Seven nations, and the European Community.*

Step 8: Encouraging Public Debate on Income Levels

Our final series of steps seeks to address both broader and more personal issues in society at large, issues that relate directly to the broad conversion required to move from a tunnel society to a tree society, or to an economy of care.

Research has demonstrated that satisfaction about the level of one's own income depends to a high degree on income distribution as a whole. This confirms the experience and feelings of many people that the importance of their income level is relative. The same research has shown that we lose two-thirds of every income increase because our needs level "floats" along with our rising level of consumption.

The question then arises of what sense it makes to continually emphasize the importance of economic growth and the accompanying increases in personal income. We propose as our eighth step that *society discuss the possibility and desirability of accepting public standards for the maximum level of earnings possible for a given job or occupation.* While this discussion ought naturally to take place in the industrialized countries of the North, it could also positively influence the debate in the South

8. Ibid., 401-55.

151

about the self-aggrandizement of the elite occurring there. Such a discussion will focus broader attention on the quality of life, especially the quality of the environment, of work, and of our relationships with the poor. It will also help to deliver us from the game of endlessly introducing new products for consumption by means of securing the highest possible incomes. In many cases such incomes barely satisfy our material desires, much less the subsistence needs of people and the environment. If we introduce a public standard that sets a limit on private earnings, then we have introduced a means by which to extricate ourselves from the jaws of the acquisitive society.

To this end, we must discuss and implement proposals in the direct sphere of income and income relationships. But we must also do the same in the indirect sphere of taxes and subsidies. That is, as we noted above, we must manage taxation policy in such a way that it helps to remedy today's economic dilemmas. Establishing public standards for a maximum level of income or consumption could retard the development of what years ago economist Jan Tinbergen called "non-sense" products.

Step 9: Assessing "Modern" Technology

Growth mania in the West and now even in Eastern Europe has reached such a pitch that it is difficult to discuss the destructive aspects of modern-day technological innovations. One often hears the retort: "But we can't go back to the Middle Ages!"

Yet we live in a society where highly skilled labor, the kind of labor that can contribute to one's sense of fulfillment in life, becomes increasingly redundant as "modern" technology helps us to achieve higher productivity. We even label this development "progress." And it often seems that employees in today's industrial society want to quit their jobs as soon as they possibly can.

Who today actually cares about the one who must put up with such labor, or the one who is expelled from the labor force? The science of economics has demonstrated little interest in the intrinsic value of work. Conversely, today's economy shows little interest in those who fall *outside* of the labor process. Further, it is striking that many economists simply accept the ongoing development of technology as a given, a datum to which all of us must simply adapt.

Indeed, the "self-evidence" of this principle forms one of the most essential trademarks of today's tunnel society, a society whose signature is the need to endlessly step up the productivity of all of its members.

The objection that arises is that perhaps we have no options available. Because of the reigning growth mania and tunnel vision, many people consider the argument already settled: the only choices before us are to go forward or backward — and who among us wants to return to the past? But consider the thesis that technological development, with all of its possibilities, is actually suited more to the image of a tree than to that of an infinitely expanding straight line. Every technologist will agree in principle that at any given moment the technological development of a society can take one of several different courses. The technologist will further acknowledge that society does not pursue every possible technological course, if only for the simple reason that not all technological possibilities garner enough financial return. In truth, technological development in the affluent nations of the North has traveled along a very narrow, one-dimensional track, a track that represents only one of a whole gamut of possibilities that we have barely explored.

Consequently, redirecting current technological possibilities away from a tunnel society and toward a tree society — thus implementing better precare for people and the environment, including encouraging human creativity in the work process — takes on essential significance. But this redirection can occur only after we have created the economic room for it (see Step 2) and have defined the responsibility of industry more broadly than we do now (Step 3). We must also fill a scientific vacuum. For where is the science that has assumed responsibility for developing "technology with a human face"? This phrase was coined by E. F. Schumacher, the British/German mining expert who in 1974 published a book with the subtitle *Economics as if People Mattered.*[9] In our reading of this book, Schumacher elaborated on the approach mapped out by the World Council of Churches in 1948. The report of the World Council's Assembly held in Amsterdam that year contains this sentence: "Humanity is not created for production, but production for humanity."

Schumacher's argument consists of locating and implementing

9. E. F. Schumacher, *Small Is Beautiful* (London: Abacus, 1974).

153

an intermediate technology. He formulated the need for this in these terms:

> There is nothing in the experience of the last twenty-five years to suggest that modern technology, as we know it, can really help us to alleviate world poverty, not to mention the problem of unemployment which already reaches levels like thirty per cent in many so-called developing countries, and now threatens to become endemic also in many of the rich countries.[10]

Similarly, this statement of Schumacher's has paramount significance for economists:

> The development of an intermediate technology . . . means a genuine forward movement into new territory, where the enormous cost and complication of production methods for the sake of labour saving and job elimination is avoided and technology is made appropriate for labour surplus societies.[11]

With the word "cost," Schumacher underscores the enormous social costs of the ever-expanding deployment of modern technology in the production process, costs that modern economists virtually ignore. These costs include pollution and the depletion of topsoil and ecosystems. But they also include the increasing risks to people's health caused by the ways in which we organize work in factories and offices and distribute work overall. It is critical that these costs become calculated into production costs in the directly productive sector. If people lament the high costs of government workers' compensation programs, then we must also investigate why hundreds of thousands of workers are physically unable to work.

In short, given the multitude of compelling reasons, we must focus considerable attention on scaling to their appropriate size the technologies and technological development that now appear to dictate our society's production methods.

To this end, we must give technological assessments more prominence in our society. But we must also muster the courage to guide technological devel-

10. Ibid., 123.
11. Ibid., 156.

*opments to their appropriate scale. In doing so, we will assure more labor input
and thereby more human creativity, and we will exercise less pressure on the
environment and its raw materials.*

Finally, we may not be satisfied simply with having the governments of the industrialized West address the issues of technological
assessment and guidance. This will even lead to mistakes if the impetus for addressing the scale of technology has not come from the
bottom up, as it were.

We see it as critical for the assessment and guidance of technological development that firms and organizations strengthen the content and quality of the voice of labor in their endeavors. We are
gratified to see that in the Netherlands, for example, trade unions have
taken an initial step toward assessing and guiding technological developments — even though the emphasis still lies too heavily on scaling
down only those technological developments that originate outside of
the country. But we commend this example to all as a significant first
step. Each year our governments in the West contribute extensive
amounts of resources to the development of new products and production methods. We urge our governments to use these resources
to foster the development of intermediate technologies, as recommended by Schumacher. In other words, we urge that our governments' incentive structure support those technological developments
that reflect a sensitivity to the *total* costs of production.

Step 10: Building a Network

In the foregoing we have submitted that today's faith in economic
growth has roots in our culture itself. Our culture exhibits a widespread belief that economic growth, meaning an increase in production, increases human well-being. Our culture therefore sees
economic growth as a sign of progress. But we believe that there is
reason to doubt that this rather unqualified growth has always brought
increasing prosperity or that it will always do so.

We are aware that reasonable doubt about a misplaced faith in
economic growth has drastic consequences for the norms and values
held in our society. It is our contention that we cannot divorce change
in the economy and in economic science from change in our culture's
deeply held convictions and values. Economic theory and practice

always reflect the intentions of a culture, and, conversely, economic theory and practice influence the culture itself.

This means that our proposals draw in many noneconomic issues. This in turn implies that we must seek advice on the changes envisioned and involve interested persons from all walks of life, people who are not necessarily trained in economics. We therefore recommend building up a network of movements and persons who wish to embrace economic renewal. Here, in the light of our own place, we think of churches, ecclesiastical organizations, congregations and parishes, women's organizations, and academicians in many fields. Further, we must also make contacts and connections with those who envision a similar renewal but who do so from out of a different basic orientation. The search for a new humanity always points us to each other. We speak in the hope that in the near future the peace, environment, and development organizations will strengthen their mutual interaction and network.

An important aid for their mutual cooperation lies in the fact that all of these organizations take their starting point in what Hannah Arendt has called the threatened human condition: they seek to draw every movement away from the precipice beyond which we violate the human condition and back to the political and economic center of our society, where decisions are made that are so critical for our well-being and our future.

Now that we have more insight into the harshness of today's economic system, we must speak together and without fear about our own positions. *Organizations and movements devoted to care for the future of the environment and of human society should therefore consult with one another about possible directions to follow, even if that means subjecting our own patterns of life to the scrutiny of others.*

Step 11: Assessing International Trade Agreements

Nations do not stand alone. Economically and politically they participate in larger blocs and interest groups. The North American Free Trade Agreement (NAFTA) and the recently completed General Agreement on Trade and Tariffs (GATT) represent two such blocs. Blocs such as these often cannot simply follow whatever path they please. Rather, they often form pure expressions of the material self-interests they represent and of communities that remain closed to broader objectives.

A striking example of the dilemmas that emerge in these contexts arises out of the recent history of Europe. In 1989 the boundary of stone dividing East and West Berlin fell. And 1992 was selected as the year in which the European Community would collapse the economic boundaries between its member states. These events seem to have developed along identical lines and thus to have reinforced each other. But upon closer examination, we detect a stark contrast. For though the fall of the Berlin Wall was a sign of the embrace of East and West, the collapse of economic boundaries, if the indications are correct, will launch a period in which the affluent Western European states will seek to curtain off the East and the South.

We realize of course that the predictions of many others sound different. Likewise, the official explanations by political leaders in Western Europe suggest that a renewed European Community will seek more cooperation with the countries of Eastern Europe and apply itself more vigorously to environmental and Third World interests. But we question the realism of these predictions, for at least two reasons.

First, policy resolutions of this nature involve not only what people intend but also what lies in the realm of possibility. Time after time in past years the powerful lobbies of the European Community's own interest groups, whether of the farming, auto, transportation, or chemical industries, appear to have exercised much more control over de facto policy than did stirring appeals voiced by the Third World, appeals that included urgent requests to free up imports and not to dump food surpluses from the European Community's agricultural production. They also have carried more weight than did pleas by environment organizations to institute a common policy on a number of pressing global ecological problems, and they have even outmuscled appeals from former East bloc countries to unite with the European Community. Time and time again the Minister's Council of the European Economic Community has appeared to allow national agricultural and industrial interests to prevail over any recommendation for instituting a responsible international policy. Even the most artificial tariff barriers blocking the access of the poor countries to the European Community have remained untouched. If this has been true in the past, then why will the future be any different?

Secondly, here, too, a *structural* problem plays a significant role. Since the European Community was founded by means of the Treaty of Rome in 1957, the formulation of the objectives laid out in the treaty have remained unaltered. In the Treaty of Maastricht, a few new objectives have merely been added to the existing ones. Thus article 2 of the Treaty of Rome, which formulates the basis of the European Community, remains fully in force. It states: "The Community shall have as its task . . . to promote throughout the Community a harmonious development of economic activities, a continuous and balanced expansion . . . and an accelerated raising of the standard of living."[12] The goal of material economic progress still forms the heart of the European Community, while social policy, environmental policy, and development policy merely "flank" the current economic order. They possess no real corrective power.

What then must be done if the European Community is to display signs of a just and sustainable society, instead of a society that serves to enrich the affluent nations even further? At the very least, the European Community must express in clear terms its ecological and international responsibilities. These may not serve as objectives "coordinated" with objectives promoting economic growth, but as tasks that expressly limit the material economic desires of the citizens and member states of the European Community. If this does not occur, then we fear that the European Commission will not have a leg to stand on when conflict arises with the Minister's Council of the European Community.

Perhaps, then, the European experience contains a lesson for North America. To the extent that NAFTA does not possess clear, minimum social and environmental provisions — provisions that expressly limit the material economic desires of North Americans — the economic processes stimulated by NAFTA will run roughshod over sound environmental and social policies. The reason is that the countries with the lowest environmental and social standards will hold the competitive advantage! To make matters worse, this advantage will have the effect of exerting downward pressure on the social and environmental standards that already exist in member states of the trading bloc. This phenomenon, known as ecological and social

---

12. Amos J. Paeslee, ed., *International Governmental Organizations: Constitutional Documents,* 5 vols. (The Hague: Martinus Nijhoff, 1974), 1:458.

"dumping," shows that the formation of international trading blocs built for the primary purpose of material advancement is an irresponsible policy in our time.

We therefore fully endorse United States Vice President Al Gore's proposal that "governments should require the incorporation of standards to protect the environment in treaties and international agreements," with the proviso that social standards be included.[13]

In general, at the outset, as citizens we ought to test every new form of political and economic cooperation with the criteria of social and environmental sustainability and of a genuine openness to the participation of "weaker" states. If we do not do so, then any new forms of international economic cooperation will inevitably assist only in closing the loop of the tunnel society.

Step 12: Western Life-style

If a single theme has characterized this book, it is that if we are to resolve today's pressing local and global economic impasses, then our actions and ways of life must change. Thus it is no accident that we conclude our series of steps with an appeal to alter our life-style. This appeal does not entail simply taking on certain social obligations on behalf of others and our immediate environment. Rather, it involves developing a way of life that is content with "enough" and that demonstrates this contentment by a conscious acceptance of a level of income and consumption that does not escalate. Let us therefore state most emphatically that the appeal to alter our life-style does *not* consist of urging us to make painful "sacrifices" for the sake of others. On the contrary, our appeal is fundamentally different in principle. It involves the realization that because of our collective drive for more and more, we directly damage our *own* well-being. W require another vision of life, a vision in which the word "enough" plays a positive role. The implementation of such a vision will create new possibilities for *neighborliness,* for demonstrating *care for our surroundings,* and for having more *time* available in our harried lives. Such a vision will help to liberate not only the poor but also the *rich.*

In this respect, the consumption patterns of many people in the

13. Al Gore, *Earth in the Balance* (New York: Houghton Mifflin Company, 1992), 346-47.

West deserve more attention. The need for responsible consumption remains very real. Of course, life-style issues contain a personal element. But they also speak to the responsibility we hold in common for the consumption patterns of our culture. Fashion, for example, exercises considerable influence in many areas today, not just clothing. Resisting certain fashion tendencies is not just a matter of personal consumption but also of group and societal consumption. We must develop fashion practices other than those forced upon us by advertising and commerce.

Similarly, the peculiar passion by which many of us undermine our own health by using tobacco or alcohol (a passion often rooted in societal problems) carries over into our eating habits. Eating disorders, such as bulimia and anorexia, plague only affluent societies, and they have mushroomed in our time. Binswanger and his Swiss colleagues have shown that eating practices today are a form of premature depletion of our bodies. According to estimates, Germany pays 3 billion marks each year in social assistance moneys for diseases that relate in some way to unhealthy nourishment. The West's problem is *over*eating.

A second critical area where alteration of our contemporary life-style is required is the increasing lack of time in our busy lives. Many people seem to have lost the realization that continually escalating levels of consumption put greater pressure on the time available to us, because more consumption means that more of our time is tied up with products and goods. But if we wish to live in a culture in which human contact has a central place (indeed, this is a singular condition for the preservation of any culture), then we must free up the time that we now increasingly use with products and goods. The well-being of people therefore is not strictly linked with expanding our possessions, and when an industrialized culture opts to continually elevate its material prosperity it does so at the expense of the increasing loneliness and isolation of its members. People simply have less time for each other.

Therefore, in all areas, including education, we must promote the notion that human well-being, both of ourselves and of others, requires first and foremost a life-style of restraint, not luxury. And to achieve a sustainable economy, as consumers we must fight the throwaway mentality and put value on secondhand goods.

*   *   *

A sense of abundance can arise only if we have a sense of enough, for abundance is the awareness of having more than enough. Yet in the realm of scarcity in which we live, it is precisely the awareness of abundance that we as a society are steadily losing. Perhaps taking steps in the direction of an economy of care, or an economy of enough, will help us to regain our diminishing sense of abundance.

Together, these twelve steps outline a way or path to follow. They need not be taken in the precise order described here, and they leave room for all sorts of variations. But considered as a whole, they help to define a movement that draws us away from the dark abyss that our society is now perilously approaching. The path outlined here — together with whatever amendments and changes are appropriate — therefore cannot be lightly dismissed. For it contains a choice, a choice in direct contrast to the ongoing deadly cycle of self-enrichment and self-destruction. At its most basic level, it contains a choice for life itself, and for the One who has given all of us life.

Index